THE SEASONAL
COCKTAIL
COMPANION

THE SEASONAL

COCKTAIL

COMPANION

100

RECIPES & PROJECTS
for 4 Seasons of Drinking

MAGGIE SAVARINO

SASQUATCH
BOOKS

Printed in the United States of America
Published by Sasquatch Books
17 16 15 14 13 12 11   9 8 7 6 5 4 3 2 1

Cover design and illustrations: Anna Goldstein
Interior design and composition: Sarah Plein
Interior photographs: Jim Henkens and Christopher Nelson
Interior illustrations: Diana Prince

Library of Congress Cataloging-in-Publication Data is available.

ISBN-13: 978-1-57061-755-3
ISBN-10: 1-57061-755-4

Sasquatch Books
119 South Main Street, Suite 400
Seattle, WA 98104
(206) 467-4300
www.sasquatchbooks.com
custserv@sasquatchbooks.com

for Kim Ricketts
∽ my friend, mentor, and the person responsible ⤳
for this book in at least 27 different ways

∿ **Contents** ∾

PART ONE: THE BASICS

PART TWO: THE SEASONS

~ **Acknowledgments** ~

To the friends and family that made this book possible, especially:

My daily cohorts, Cormac Mahoney, Bryan Jarr, and Zoi Antonitsas, for their utmost tolerance, as well as that of the rest of the Madison Park Conservatory staff.

———

Whitney Ricketts, dearest friend and editor, for gerrymandering the ideas that are now on the next 200 pages and talking me down from some ledges and onto the right ones.

———

My brother Matt, sister-in-law Teresa, and parents John and Kathy Wysocki, for unmeasured support in all things.

———

⤳ Introduction ⤵

You are not a bartender. But those of us behind the bar are not magicians or alchemists. We have the benefit of endless repetition and brains barnacled with crib sheets, flavor profiles, ratios, and experience to guide us when making a drink. We just know more than you do. And that's OK. My accountant knows more than I do about depreciation schedules as a pianist knows a song in many keys. It just so happens that a bartender's trade is more applicable to daily life. Cocktail recipes are my depreciation schedules, and I'm more fun at parties.

Myriad bar books exist that will give you recipes handed down through the decades and new recipes that are really just slight variations on the old. You probably have one of those books already. The focus of this book is to help you screw around with the basics.

Wonderful things can happen when you tinker with a drink recipe. On the other hand, I strongly believe that tradition matters as an anchor. Recipes have value. No matter how the cocktail's been bastardized, for example, I still believe that a martini without vermouth is just a glass of chilled white liquor with some olives in it. It's about the fundamentals. You can make a lifetime's worth of drinks riffing on the eleven basic cocktails on page 178, for example.

Don't get discouraged because you're not a bartender; just start with the basics and experiment on your friends. Making drinks at home allows you to do things far too tedious for bars to do—like soaking cinnamon, apples, and pears in vermouth to add to a batch of something that might once have resembled a manhattan but now is the official drink of your weekend.

If I do my own taxes, I can get audited. If you monkey around with a cocktail recipe, what's the worst that can happen? Nothing ice, soda, and a lime can't fix.

Remember: It's not the last drink you're ever going to make.

The bar isn't the only place to find inspiration. If you like dark or aged rum, for example, look in cookbooks and online for desserts and other dishes using rum or for foods that remind you of the flavors in rum—toffee and caramel, for example. See what fruits and spices go into a dish, and play around with them in a glass.

The best way to learn how to make a good cocktail—other than repeating it behind a bar nightly for hours—is to look at it as you would salad dressing.

When you make your own salad dressing, when your pantry is set up with a few different vinegars and you have a decent condiment collection, you wonder why you ever relied solely on the store-bought stuff when you can make something that is exactly to your taste (more on this in Adjuncts, page 45). It doesn't make store-bought dressing bad; it just means you can have something at home that is all you— not so much balsamic vinegar or maybe none at all, half Dijon and half brown mustard.

That's the point of this book—to help you find the things you like to go with the things you know. I adapted these recipes from those I've used in bars over the years, abbreviating them for the home drinker in the interest of time, ingredients, and effort. Hardly any of the recipes here are too precious to avoid further alteration. Again, you're making salad dressing, not a soufflé. Alcohol is very forgiving.

Everything here is to taste. My worship for cardamom knows no end, for example, but I've spared you most of this love. You might find yourself throwing cinnamon sticks in everything. If a final product— drink or infusion—doesn't quite work for you, change it. If an infusion is too sour for your taste, add simple syrup. If it's too sweet, add citrus or moderate it with more booze. If it's too bitter, OK, you may have to cook with it.

This book favors seasonal ingredients as well as ingredients in the spirit of a certain season, but don't let it be overbearing. If you want to make peach bitters in February, go nuts. Every grocery store has a freezer stocked with fruit, so let's none of us pretend we live in such a rarified world.

Nothing here counts as world-ending, and the only thing you should cry over is spilt whiskey.

I hope you use this book in fits and starts. I hope you set an afternoon aside to zest a mountain of grapefruit and put herbs and spices in jars with various boozes, with friends in mind and Dixie Blues on the stereo. I hope you hunt around for a few friendly looking pages to make a thing or two to complement your favorite bottle of rye whiskey. I hope you find a way to translate your love of Caesar salad into something that will kill Bloody Marys for all time . . . at least at your house. Use what you know and be inspired by what you see and what you already like.

But most of all, I hope you take it only so seriously.

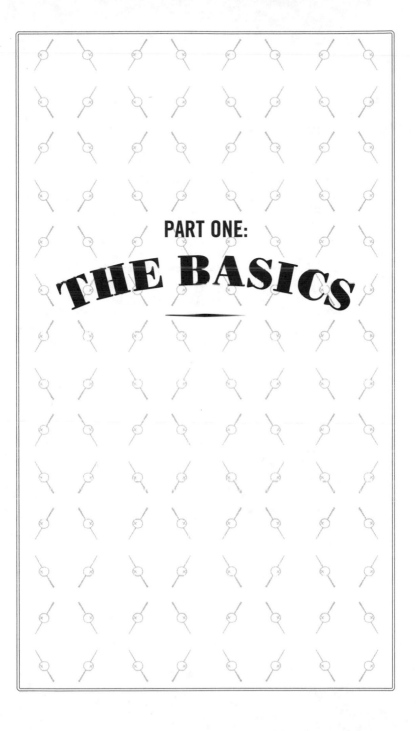

PART ONE:
THE BASICS

Botanicals,
∼ Herbs & Spices ∼

Making the recipes in this book requires one, and only one, big step from you: being proactive about your ingredients, especially your spice-buying habits. And by proactive I mean that you can still order them online at home in your underwear, but old spice is for aftershave, not for any recipe in this book. The following ingredients impart flavor and aroma through the volatile chemicals and oils contained in their leaves, seeds, flowers, and other parts. *Volatile*, when referring to a chemical or oil, signifies that which can evaporate. Smell a piece of mint, all fresh and light and clean. Now tear it and rub it between your fingers. Now the aroma is intense because you've released the volatile oil within the leaf. This is what happens when we drink and chew. Volatile chemicals reach up through the nasal cavity where they are detected and identified . . . and we taste them.

SMELL IS TASTE

In Adjuncts (see page 45) I deal with the four basic tastes: sweet, salty, bitter, and sour. Flavor is a combination of these tastes, along with smell. Most of what we taste actually comes from what we smell. Think of the last time you had a nasty head cold; could you taste what you ate? The basic tastes register on different parts of the tongue and combine with specific volatile chemicals and oils in herbs, spices, and food to produce in our brains the impression of the flavor of a piece of licorice or a pork chop or a strawberry.

When you make an infusion, you are trying to capture these chemicals, either by leeching them out of their homes with alcohol or by steeping them out in hot water as you would brew tea. To make a good infusion, you want to work with ingredients that have lost as little of their volatile components as possible. That's why it's good to empty out the spice cupboard every few months, especially since it is normally close to the stove; heat and moisture speed up the evaporation of all that is volatile in spices and herbs. The less volatile the chemicals, the less the flavor.

SMELL IS MEMORY

Humans can detect thousands of smells, and science still can't tell us exactly how we do it. We are talking animals who at one point depended upon the sense of smell to survive—detecting predators on the wind and food in the forest and that which was putrid or poisonous. Each of us will have a strong reaction to a handful of the botanicals used in these recipes because smell triggers memory like none of our other senses. There's a reason a good realtor will throw a baking sheet of chocolate chip cookies in the oven during an open house, and who among us hasn't been tempted by the siren smell of Cinnabon at the airport or mall? It's Pavlovian—except the bell is cinnamon.

Different smell memories and sensitivities no doubt will lead you to adjust a thing or two in these recipes. There's always room for the memory if you just can't get enough anise seed. I dialed down a bit all measurements for anise-related spices because of my selfish aversion to its pungency. So when I say everything is a personal choice, I mean it. No two of us smells or tastes things the same way. We are each our own Goldilocks with a singular concept of "just right."

PROCUREMENT AND STORAGE

If you want to make your own spice blend or curry, use the freshest spices and herbs possible. Buying directly from a reputable local or online spice merchant (see page 23) is the best way to ensure freshness and quality of botanicals. Fresh herbs and flowers should be used immediately, and with herbs a little bruising just before infusing or boiling coaxes essential oils and compounds from their surfaces.

Supermarkets carry a limited variety of fresh herbs, and most Asian specialty groceries will carry the more eccentric herbs used in these recipes. Of course, herbs are as easy to grow as having a windowsill and a pot to put them in. If you find you have an affinity for one or two of the more unique greens in this book, think about them as your next houseplants that pay dividends. Nurseries and select home improvement stores carry starters and seeds year-round.

Spices can be kept for a few months if you use airtight containers. Use small stickers to date your containers to keep track of freshness.

Fresh herbs should be rinsed and dried in a salad spinner or rolled in a towel. Try to remove as much surface moisture as possible. You can pick your herbs, discarding the stems or using them as you would chives in cooking; it's a matter of preference and finickiness regarding the green flavor and lack of desirable volatiles in most stems.

AN ANNOYING DISCLAIMER

There's no definitive *Western* medical evidence proving the efficacy of herbs and spices against certain diseases or their effective use in treatment for what ails you. Information is presented to provide historical context, not to prescribe. The FDA would want me to say that. So there. I said it. But then, chamomile doesn't advertise on television or have a lobbyist, and millions of grandmothers through the centuries can't always be wrong. So I said that, too. Moving on . . .

I can't lie to you. I freak over coriander and cardamom and mace blades, my newest crush used for the first time for this book while researching historic *falernum* recipes (see page 168). Many recipes have ingredients chosen for my preferences in aroma and flavor, and also for the name's sake. For what's in a name? I'd submit "grains of paradise" for your consideration.

Lady's Mantle, or "A Cautionary Tale"

Over its three decades of existence, Tenzing Momo, in the Pike Place Market, has become a one-stop shop for the alterna-minded, with tarot cards, incense, magical oils, all-natural remedies, and bath products. But it can function as more than just a pit stop for vacationing hippies or angst-ridden teen witches if you let it— herbal sommeliers comprise the store's staff. Normally the sight of prayer flags and the smell of incense repel me, but the store's herbs and other products, along with the knowledgeable service, have made Tenzing Momo part of my regular routine.

I first frequented Tenzing Momo for custom herbal tea—which the staff gladly helps customers devise—and I became hooked on the store when I began to rely on it for all the awesomely named supplies I need for my homemade bitters. The shop has herbs that very few spice markets carry, like horehound and orrisroot (smells like violets), and comes off as far less intimidating than an apothecary that specializes in Chinese herbs, if only for the fact that you can pronounce all the words on the jars.

In the do-it-yourself world in which we live, a little bit of knowledge can be revolutionary—or dangerous. Some things should not be tried at home without consulting an expert—Google searches don't count. No matter what I've consulted the staff about, the helpful, serene counter people have never balked at even my most bizarre request and have been far more reliable than any of the conflicting information sources on the Internet.

For example, I always make my own bitters for use in cocktails and as an aid for tummy-aches. But when I first got into it fifteen years ago and I was concocting a particularly esoteric batch, I went to Tenzing Momo to pick out some of the bitter herbs that, I'm not embarrassed to say, I chose based on their names.

Good thing I checked myself before I wrecked myself. Just because herbs are natural doesn't mean they can't mess up your innards. Concentrating those herbs into homemade bitters increases the chance of discovering their side effects. Turns out that the lady's mantle I wanted to use, already an ingredient in my root beer, aids in conception (cripes!) and also isn't recommended for people taking iron supplements because it interferes with absorption (double cripes!). Skullcap, reputedly a tranquilizing herb, apparently can cause liver toxicity and shouldn't be used as casually or as regularly as I use bitters.

Though the staff members are advocates of herbs for medicinal use, they're not naturopaths, and no one will presume to diagnose or prescribe. But they will warn. So when consulting your local herbalist, always let them know your intentions.

Tenzing Momo
93 Pike Street, in the Economy Building
Seattle's Pike Place Market
www.tenzingmomo.com

⤙ The Short List ⤙

Here are forty-one herbs, flowers, and spices based on what's readily available in spice shops and online, and what's included in this book. All weight-to-volume measurements are approximate, with thanks to World Spice Merchants (www.worldspice.com) for the translations.

Allspice
Pimenta dioica
The odd name here refers to the fact that allspice has the characteristics of three spices all in one: nutmeg, cinnamon, and clove. Allspice berries are used in pickling and in cold-weather desserts, often paired with the spices it resembles. On its own it has a woody sweet spice that veers toward juniper berry. Lightly crushing the berries will release more of its clove and nutmeg side.

> USE: Add allspice when you want a more recognizable spice note, like cinnamon, or to add a background chord in bitters and vermouth.

> 1 OUNCE = ⅓ CUP

Angelica Root
Angelica archangelica
Although there's a vague citrus and evergreen chord to this plant, angelica comes from the carrot family and can echo a bit of coriander, fennel, or celery, depending on whether it's fresh or dried. Angelica is a favorite of higher-end gin and also perfume; the root can produce a calming effect from infusion of leaves and stems (fresh or dried). It is also used as a rinse to fight acne, a diuretic and digestive aid, a powder to combat athlete's foot and act as a mild insecticide, and it can do your taxes. One of those things isn't true.

> USE: In conjunction with coriander, anise, or fennel (fresh or dried), it adds complexity and floral notes to infusions.

> 1 OUNCE = 2 TABLESPOONS

Anise Seed

Pimpinella anisum

The word *anise* is often used to describe the flavor of licorice, and vice versa. One of a host of spices in many bitter liqueurs, a tincture of anise seeds can combat bloating. Arak, pastis, absinthe, ouzo, Jagermeister, and sambuca all rely, in part, on anise seed for their flavor. If you grew up in America, you might call it Good & Plenty, and you either like it or you don't. According to the studies of Dr. Alan R. Hirsch of the Smell and Taste Treatment and Research Foundation in Chicago, women are attracted to the smell of anise, especially when mixed with the smell of cucumbers or doughnuts.

> USE: Anise seed is essential for sweeter akvavit and makes a great Flavored Simple Syrup (page 49) to use with lemon-laced cocktails.

> 1 OUNCE = 4 TABLESPOONS

Basil

Ocimum basilicum

Basil is a member of the mint family and one of the most omnipresent herbs in the grocery store. It lends a fresh, green quality to infusions without an accompanying flavor that will overpower. Sometimes basil replaces mint in cocktails, like the mojito, to lend a culinary edge. So trendy.

> USE: Basil's lightly piquant, green quality can also be captured in salt to add dimension to a Bloody Mary or as a different take on any drink containing mint.

Bay Leaf

Laurus nobilis

Whole, dried bay leaves are staples for making soups, and most kitchens in America probably have a handful of years-old gray-green brittle things in the cupboard right now. A sad state for a leaf that once crowned the heads of great men. Bay leaves come from the laurel tree, but not just any laurel; mind the Latin name above or use California bay, which is stronger. Bay has a woodsy aroma and flavor, sweeter than sage with a lemon note.

> USE: A subtle flavoring for creamy dishes, bay can shine on its own, as in the Bay Leaf Liqueur (page 121), or as complexity in other infusions.

Caraway

Carum carvi

Caraway has properties veering toward the savory, like cumin, and also the sweet, like fennel. It frequently lends a piquant flavor to rye bread as well as to cheese, sausage, and pickles; and it remains an essential ingredient in many liqueurs, especially akvavit.

> USE: A quick infusion will draw out the savory side and make a base that blends well with brown liquor, especially rye. A longer infusion yields the sweeter, anise-tinged aroma and flavors, as does lightly crushing the spice before use.

1 OUNCE = 4 TABLESPOONS

Cardamom

Elettaria cardamomum

One of the most expensive spices in the world, cardamom has a singular, intense flavor that is at once peppery, warm, and sweet. Cardamom is the lead spice in traditional chai and many Indian sweets. Its aroma cloys in the same way as cinnamon does but with a citrus bent; think Earl Grey tea peppercorns. Try to get the seeds still in their green pods to assure you have true cardamom. You'll have to pick the little seeds free, but it's well worth it. You might even end up with a grinder just for cardamom, like I did.

USE: Anything cinnamon can do, cardamom can do better.

1 OUNCE = JUST UNDER A ¼ CUP (OR ⅓ CUP IF STILL IN PODS)

Celery Seed

Apium graveolens

The seeds of the celery plant give off a highly concentrated aroma of celery, just without those pretty green aromas. Spicy and only a hint of the sweet you get from fennel seed, celery seed is used most popularly in pickling, on Chicago-style hot dogs, and in Bloody Marys. Lightly crushing these seeds helps to release the essential oils, pocketed just beneath the surface.

USE: Add it to an infusion when you want a savory, a bass note, or to moderate the anise flavor of another herb or seed.

1 OUNCE = 4 TABLESPOONS

Chamomile

Matricaria recutita

Chamomile helps calm and therefore is recommended as a traditional nighttime tea to combat stress and encourage sleep. It also can help against indigestion. Parts of this plant are bitter as well as aromatic, and that counts for its inclusion in several of the world's popular bitter liqueurs. Chamomile is a flowering herb; the more whole flowers you use in your infusion, the better and truer the resulting flavor. Chamomile has a sweet, hay-like aroma that edges close to floral, and the flavor is a little bit woodsy and not unlike a light tea, such as oolong. If you use low-quality chamomile, you get the bad (dirty) smell of hay.

> USE: Add to infusions as a mild bittering agent, or use as a main ingredient to highlight its unique fragrance, as in the Chamomile Liqueur (page 141).
>
> 1 OUNCE = 1¼ CUPS

Chiles

This is as broad a category as saying "herbs," so really this is about considering the use of chiles and what they provide for flavor and heat. I could write pages on different chiles, but I'll stick to two and break the format of this section. You can investigate the rest for yourself. Because you add chiles to an infusion when you want to add heat, you have to know how much heat you will add. For this reason stay away from stupid-hot chile peppers like the habañero. I stick with jalapeño, but because a chile's heat is transferred into an infusion faster than its flavor, I supplement with Anaheim chile and let the peppers macerate for two days to one week. The result is spicy but with the garden green note of mild chiles, too.

> USE: ½ seeded jalapeño plus 1 seeded Anaheim for every 2 cups of liquor.

Cilantro/Coriander, Fresh

Coriandrum sativum

In the cuisines of the entire world today, no fresh herb is as ubiquitous as cilantro (a.k.a. coriander). The flavor of these leaves fades quickly, especially when introduced to heat or alcohol. The flavor is not as grassy as parsley and has a light and sharp lemony quality. Some people are so sensitive to a compound in the herb that they will taste soap.

USE: Substitute for a savory and spicy variant in mint cocktails, like the Mojito (page 182).

Cinnamon

Cinnamomum cassia and/or verum

No other spice holds such an imprint in our brains as cinnamon. True cinnamon (*Cinnamomum verum*) generally has a finer, complex aroma and flavor and costs a little bit more than its relative, cassia (*Cinnamomum cassia*). The recipes in this book all require sticks, and the freshest possible at that. Feel free to buy sticks labeled *cassia*, just do so from a reputable dealer to get the best stuff.

USE: It's cinnamon, the warm spice everyone knows. You know when you want it.

Coriander Seed

Coriandrum sativum

Coriander seeds have an aroma and flavor that is at once floral and spicy, with citrus zest notes. Always buy whole seeds because they lose their flavor quickly. Coriander seeds play a part in garam masala and are what gives Belgian *witbier* its signature aroma. They also factor in to the majority of pickle recipes. Try to get Indian seeds as opposed to European; they have a bigger citrus note.

USE: Coriander seeds match well with citrus and add complexity when paired with more pungent spices.

1 OUNCE = 5 TABLESPOONS

Curry Leaves
Murraya koenigii tree

In Indian stews and curries (multiple spice blends of which curry leaves are only one component), these leaves operate much in the same way as the bay leaf does. Curry leaves are worth using only if you can find them fresh. The perfume is vaguely citrus, exotic, and savory sweet. Look for the fresh leaves in good Asian specialty groceries. Use whole leaves crushed by hand.

> USE: These leaves add an awesome bass note to Flavored Simple Syrups (page 49) and Cellos (page 117), a certain *je ne sais quoi*, which is the only appropriate time to use this phrase.

Dandelion
Taraxacum officinale

The entire plant from root to flower is edible, the bitter greens used in salads and the flowers even turned into wine. You'll want to be careful where you harvest yours; know exactly the history of lawn care at your dandelion patch and steer clear of the chemically treated. Fresh dandelion makes a stellar addition to Celery Bitters (page 143), or any bitters you want to come off as herbaceous or green in quality, a highly aromatic tincture, and weird little simple syrup. It's a kissing cousin to wild chickories, to put flavor in perspective, and the aroma is like a sweeter, simpler chamomile with added brightness. If you use dried dandelion, make sure to get it from a very reputable herbalist or spice shop. You want the freshest stuff possible.

> USE: Dandelion acts as a mild bittering agent and also can contribute a yellow note (there's just no other way to put it) to infusions.
>
> 1 OUNCE DRIED = 1 CUP

Dill, Fresh and Seed

Anethum graveolens

Though found all over the world, the Nordic, Eastern European, and Russian populations freak for dill more than any others—especially with fish, potatoes, and pickles. Dill is related to fennel in all but flavor; it lacks the telltale note of anise and instead is quite savory, especially in its seeds. Compare it more to caraway. The fronds of fresh dill have a distinct fresh, spicy note, wonderful when captured in akvavit.

> USE: Fresh dill will lend its unique sharp, green taste to an infusion, and dill seed will add a savory, spicy quality that's not nearly as anise-tinged as caraway.

1 OUNCE DRIED SEED = ¼ CUP

Fennel, Fresh and Seed

Foeniculum vulgare

Fresh fennel fronds have a soft, sweet anise aroma and flavor combined with a very light and fresh green aroma similar to celery. The entire plant, frond to bulb, can be used in infusions, and it makes a charming liqueur on its own (see page 100). Licorice is not listed among these herbs and spices because fennel and anise—both star and regular—give better, more controlled results.

Fennel seed has the same aroma and flavor profile of anise seed but dialed down a few notches, which is why it is used in both sweet and savory cooking. Those little candy-coated things you see in Indian restaurants contain fennel seed, a natural breath freshener. Fennel echoes the softer note of akvavit, whereas anise seed screams ouzo.

> USE: When you want to moderate the anise flavor in an infusion, reach for fennel seed. To add a light sweet anise quality and herbal aroma, use fresh fennel.

1 OUNCE = ¼ CUP

Fenugreek Seed

Trigonella foenum-graecum

A very small and hard seed, its complex nutty and spicy aroma is worth the trouble. Known as the Greek hayseed, it has a subtle taste of fennel. Toasting it before using ups the nutty quotient. Fenugreek is a traditional ayurvedic medicine used as a laxative; it is also used as a supplement for high cholesterol and to help with metabolism and blood sugar regulation. You need a hard-core mortar and pestle for this one, or a spice grinder.

USE: Fenugreek contributes to infusions the spice equivalent of muskiness in perfume.

1 OUNCE = 4 TABLESPOONS

Gentian Root

Gentiana lutea

Otherwise known as yellow gentian, this root is pure bitterness, the same as another better-known pure bitter, angostura. If you like the aromas and flavors in a bitters you are making, you use gentian to add (more) bitterness but nothing else. Use it in small quantities and add at the end of maceration; if you leave gentian in too long, the mixture may become unpalatable.

USE: Pure plutonium-strength bitterness.

1 OUNCE = ½ CUP

Gingerroot
Zingiber officinale

The flavor of fresh, grated gingerroot has no substitute. Historically, its culinary uses were intermittently eclipsed by its medicinal use. During medieval times it was as well traded in Europe as was pepper; when ginger brew became popular in the 1800s in England, taverns sprinkled Ginger Sugar (page 56) on all sorts of drinks.

> USE: The spicy, sweet, and numbing qualities of this root play well in a syrup or infusion as long as you know that it will almost always be the star of the show.

Grains of Paradise
Afromomum melegueta

Somewhere to the left of the peppercorn but a few stops short of cardamom lies paradise. Easy to crush, these grains work very well in long infusions, when cardamom might take over the show. The grains kill the cardamom when they are freshly ground over the top of a sour or 'nog style beverage, adding an unexpected zing.

> USE: Grains of paradise are my secret weapon in many bitters recipes because they lend themselves to both sweet and savory spice mixtures.

1 OUNCE = 3½ TABLESPOONS

Hibiscus

Hibiscus sabdariffa

Hibiscus, a.k.a. sorrel in the Caribbean and Jamaica flowers in Mexico, is a flower used quite often in dried form, in aguas frescas and herbal teas. Imagine the flavor of it as cranberry in flower form. Add a handful and a few limes worth of zest to vodka, and you make an infusion that knocks the cosmopolitan on its ass.

> USE: Hibiscus is fantastic added to lemonade and white wine punch or vermouth because it lends the tanginess of cranberry with beautiful aromatics.
>
> 1 OUNCE = ¾ CUP OR MORE

Horehound

Marrubium vulgare

A few old-timey candy makers still make hard lozenge drops with this herb, known to soothe sore throats. Horehound is a bitter herb that comes off as sweet when steeped in a tea, which was recommended as a folksy cure for what ailed you. A little bit burnt caramel and a little bit wintergreen, it also snuck its way into root beers back in the day.

> USE: This herb adds a soft bitterness to infusions and a pleasant background note when combined with pungent spices such as cinnamon.
>
> 1 OUNCE = 1 CUP

Horseradish

Armoracia rusticana

The secret weapon in the Bloody Mary, horseradish root is a good source of vitamin C and—believe it or not—aids in digestion. Grating the root releases its flavor, its natural defenses. It's a clean heat that doesn't clock in with as much pain as chile peppers, but this root is a part of the mustard family (ergo, mustard gas). The active compounds can cause much sputtering and choking, which is why Bloody Marys should be ordered like Thai food, with a rating system of one to four coughs.

USE: Sparingly and for the spicy without as much tongue pain.

THE HERBAL CHEF

When I did a little side work for Seattle's Theo Chocolate—with the kindest, most amazing socially responsible and fun employees, not to mention a downright good-to-the-very-last-cocoa nib company— I got to be a small part of a collaboration with local chefs who came to our kitchen for a day to play around and make up confections. (I know, my life is a tragedy.)

Jerry Traunfeld, chef-owner of Poppy restaurant in Seattle and author of *The Herbfarm Cookbook* was one of those chefs. His final concoction: a huckleberry pâté de fruit with basil white chocolate ganache coated in dark chocolate. His book had already been an inspiration for many meals and drinks for me. Don't tell him, but I still have a copy of his wish list for the Theo chef session, about thirty ideas and various flavor combinations with different herbs and spices. To me it's like I have the original formula for Coca-Cola, and I will crib from it for years—with credit, of course. For example, any time I used anise hyssop, Jerry made me do it. And I still need to find a liquid expression of chamomile and apricot as delicate as his. . . . But I'm just a novice and all I have is his list, like a monkey with a monolith.

Hyssop
Hyssopus officinalis

Hyssop (a.k.a. anise hyssop) has been used as an aromatic since the times of jousting. Some nail it as one of the key-notes of green Chartreuse because of its high-toned, vaguely spearmint or camphor-like aroma (that's nice for VapoRub), but it also has a note similar to marjoram but far lighter. It also makes a wonderful tea when you have a cold. It is easy to grow and will bring all the bees to the yard. Search out hyssop honey for something truly spectacular.

> USE: Replace anise or mint for a milder, more complex result than either of the former.
>
> 1 OUNCE = ¾ CUP OR MORE

Jasmine
Jasminum odoratissimum

Elysian Brewing in Seattle puts jasmine flowers in the hopper with one of its ales. I'd always loved green tea with jasmine, but that beer made me think. The fragrance and mild flavor of jasmine is sexy and singular. Fresh flowers are kept with dried tea to absorb the oils, but dried flowers can still lend a heady aroma.

> USE: Start sparingly to scent simple syrup, or make a tincture for adding to drinks in the same way you would orange flower water or in a simple dry gin martini.
>
> 1 OUNCE = ¾ CUP

Juniper Berries
Juniperus communis
The key flavoring agent in many gins and what gave gin its name, juniper berries are the epitome of pine but sweet and with a hint of citrus. Like camphor, they aid in digestion and bronchial problems. The freshest dried berries will have a far greater complexity than ones that have been sitting around.

> USE: In small amounts, juniper berries add a high note to infusions and pair well with lemon and seeds from the carrot family (fennel, dill, caraway, anise).
>
> 1 OUNCE = ⅓ CUP

Lavender Flowers
Lavandula spica
More than just for bubble bath, lavender is an important ingredient in the popular French spice mix herbes de Provence. This is another ingredient some people have great sensitivity to, so I try to make a lavender tincture and add it to infusions ex post facto much of the time. Also, try adding more lavender for a shorter period of time at the very end of an infusion. In a half-torn herb book I have from the 1800s, it says applying a lavender cold compress to the head "relieves giddiness." Just know: In an infusion, it has the opposite effect.

> USE: Combine it with other spices to moderate its floral note, or highlight it specifically.
>
> 1 OUNCE = 1 CUP

Lemongrass

Cymbopogon citratus

Part of the holy troika of Thai cuisine, lemongrass pieces look like stiff green onions morphing into bamboo. Like a leek or green onion, remove a layer of the stiff outer coating and cut stalks down to about the bottom two-thirds. You don't have to skin these down as far as you would in cooking because you're going for maximum aromatics. Use the leaves, too, if they are attached. The aroma of lemongrass, not uncommon in herbal tea, is at once literal to its name and more perfumed than its name suggests, almost floral. It goes best in vodka, in summer, and on the deck. Don't waste your time with the dried stuff.

> USE: It's a little bit lemony and a little bit mint and perfume; substitute or add it accordingly, except in a mojito, when you'd be left chewing its bits for days.

¼ CUP = ONE 6-INCH PORTION OF STALK, CHOPPED

Lemon Verbena

Lippia triphylla

You've got to be careful with this fresh herb. For many it smells only of furniture polish. The aroma does have a weight to it; it's related to Mexican oregano and smells like a cross between it and lemon rind. The plant is extremely easy to grow in a pot or herb garden. Use the fresh whole leaves.

> USE: Sneak it into drinks using gin or those that call for citrus.

SOURCING THE SPICE

If you don't have a spice merchant or reputable, super fresh bulk foods provider near you, use mine.

When I came back from Spain years ago with a pea in my mattress about a certain spice I had in sautéed chickpeas—the single greatest thing I ate on that trip—World Spice Merchants quickly diagnosed my new crush, sniffing me through four spice blends before nailing *ras al hanout*, still the official spice blend of my house. And it's here I learned the aroma properties and uses of chiles I've never heard of, which beat randomly buying things at the Mexican grocery in the market to various painful ends.

"If you're buying spice in the small bulk section of your grocery store or from a place that doesn't necessarily specialize, you get what they have. Here, if you want cinnamon you have seven different choices, and we're sourcing the freshest and best spice we can," says Erin Handly, the shop's manager. She advises a smell test when at all possible. "It's such a cliché, but your nose really does know all. We may not use it as much in modern life, but we're still animals. If you have to think about what you're smelling or wait for it to hit you, the spice is too old. When you smell fresh spice, it's like smelling a great wine; you may not know what it is, but you know it's something special. Our fresh fennel seed has so much nuance that many people never get to enjoy if they're buying the stuff that's already months old in a tiny jar at the grocery store."

She's right. the fennel I get when mixed with a little fresh bulb is like a church organ compared to a Casio keyboard.

World Spice Merchants has lower minimum orders than some online providers (by the ounce), and you can throw in an airtight jar for another $2—one-stop shopping. Having used them to ship spices to family and friends, I know that they deal in the highest-quality, freshest stuff, and I couldn't have written this book without them.

World Spice Merchants
1509 Western Avenue
Seattle's Pike Place Market
www.worldspice.com

Mace Blades

Myristica fragrans tree

A tree with two spices, the *Myristica fragrans* produces fruit. The seed of that fruit is nutmeg, and the meat that surrounds the seed is mace. Mace blades are pale little pieces of spice jerky that usually become part of pumpkin pie spice blend. Whole mace blades possess a far more subtle spice than nutmeg, though related.

> USE: Throw away your clove. These blades create a fog of aroma when used in an infusion, surrounding the other aromas and flavors. Also, it's the coolest spice name ever.

1 OUNCE = ⅔ CUP

Makrut Lime Leaf

Citrus hystrix

Widely known as kaffir lime leaf, these leaves come from the makrut lime. Efforts are being made to reclaim that term; the word *kaffir* is an offensive term in parts of Africa. The little waxy leaves have a distinctive smell of sweet citrus, green, and flowers that borders on intoxicating (I limit my use of this word to just this once, so you know I mean it), a perfume fit for Mama Nature herself. A flavoring in so much Southeast Asian cuisine, find it fresh in Asian specialty groceries, or keep your own dwarf tree. You can buy them online; they need only a sunny place and will make the house smell insanely good.

> USE: These lime leaves deepen the flavor and aroma of anything containing citrus and make an outrageous infusion for rum.

Nigella Seed
Nigella damascena
Outside of coming from the coolest-looking plant that can't kill you,
a nigella seed tastes like a peppercorn that slept in an herb patch and
has onion breath.

USE: Fantastic cracked on top of breads and pastas, it adds
punch to an infusion as well as a very mild bitterness.

1 OUNCE = ¼ CUP

Pandan Leaf
Pandanus amaryllifolius
Pandan leaf has a light musky and heady quality similar to almond
butter or milk taffy and is very mild. Some put the smell closer to
vanilla. In Southeast Asia and India, pandan leaves flavor many sweets,
rice puddings, and cakes. Use the whole leaves, which you can find in
Asian specialty groceries either fresh or frozen fresh.

USE: For long infusions, pandan leaves add a sweet, warm spice
(and light green tint) without overtaking the other ingredients.
They are also a fantastic flavoring for sugar.

Peppermint
Mentha piperita
So common yet so varied in flavor, mint can be taken for granted. The
culinary mint you find in the grocery store is often a mild peppermint,
meant for as wide a range of uses as possible. But mint grows like a
weed and will fill a pot or barrel in no time. So if you plant only a few
herbs, mint pays amazing dividends, and you can find one that suits
your specific tastes.

USE: Try substituting spearmint (*Mentha spicata*) and its
cooler, softer flavor in a julep or syrup. Fresh mint can help
moderate warmer spice flavors and bittering agents in tinctures.

Rosebuds and/or Rose Petals

Rosa centifolia

All roses are edible, but you want to make sure what you use are "culinary grade" roses, meaning they have not been treated with chemicals. If not explicitly listed as such, ask the spice merchant. It's also OK to cheat and use rose water in recipes; sometimes you're not sure how rosy you want an infusion. Use whole buds or petals, fresh or dried.

USE: Any time you want to add some sexy.

1 OUNCE = ¾ CUP DRIED FLOWERS

Rosemary

Rosmarinus officianlis

Rosemary smells like a Northwest forest—wood, pine, and sweet camphor notes. The aroma is beyond pungent for some, just like juniper berries. It really doesn't matter whether you use dry or fresh rosemary because the plant seems to reek, no matter its state. Citrus takes well to a little rosemary; just watch the dosage. A tincture of rosemary oil is said to improve circulation.

USE: Rosemary gives off a zesty pine note that plays well with lemon and as part of a chord with other savory herbs, allspice, or juniper.

1 OUNCE = ½ CUP LEAVES (NEEDLES)

Sage

Salvia officinalis

First, make sure to use culinary sage because there are tons of different varieties. Pineapple sage is the most desirable variety for infusing and nonsavory cooking. It has a fruity aroma, backed by the earthy, wood pine and citrus backbone of the herb, and as a member of the mint family, some varieties have a vague trace of mint. Use whole fresh leaves, which can be dried to further moderate influence.

USE: A wonderful component in peach bitters, experiment with using sage along with tree and stone fruits. (Think about fruits associated with Thanksgiving as a start . . .)

Sarsaparilla

Smilax regelii

Sarsaparilla is one of the gang of flavorings that became fashionable during the soft drink rush of the 1800s, alongside root beers and colas and even spawning a splinter group of soft drinks named after it. After sassafras was reported to be a carcinogen, sarsaparilla replaced it as a root beer ingredient. Sarsaparilla has a bitter taste and sweet smell, softly wintergreen backed by a little warm spice. It is a mild bittering agent, but care should still be taken not to leave it in an infusion for too long.

> USE: Great paired with cinnamon and lime; use it to add depth to berry infusions and syrups.
>
> 1 OUNCE = 1¼ CUPS

Star Anise

Illicum verum

Make sure the jar has a wide enough mouth for this star-shaped spice; it would be a shame to break off its gorgeous points. Completely unrelated to the European variety, star anise has a similar aroma and flavor to anise because of a shared chemical compound, but far less sharp and warmer when used in infusions.

> USE: In place of or in conjunction with cinnamon, nutmeg, or cardamom.
>
> 1 OUNCE = APPROXIMATELY ⅓ CUP

Sweetgrass

Hierochloe oderata

Also known as bison grass, the subtle aroma is much like far-faded vanilla with a slightly sweet fennel edge. I am including it because of its prevalence in the northern states. Sweetgrass plays a part in Native American ceremonies and crafts. Use fresh, clean leaves. Sweetgrass may be purchased as a ground cover from garden centers.

USE: See page 121 for a homemade take on the unique Polish vodka infusion Zubrowka.

Vanilla Bean

Vanilla fragrans

Some recipes in this book refer to "spent" vanilla beans. That means you've used them once but they still have life in them. When you put a new vanilla bean in an infusion, it will take over the bottle and then the world. Think about vanilla extract; smells good, tastes like crap. But if the bean has been used once, it will give just the right amount of vanilla for your infusion. Look for Mexican vanilla beans to save some money; although considered less fine in the world of pastry chefs, they work like champs in booze for far fewer pesos.

USE: Vanilla is the spice equivalent of bacon. You can put it in just about anything, but that doesn't mean it necessarily belongs. It's a personal choice.

ᐁ Equipment & Prep ᐁ

No need to get remedial here. I assume if you're old enough to drink, you're grown-up and settled down enough to own some basic kitchen equipment.

The recipes in this book require a few extra items to start you on your way, mostly for straining and storing. None of the equipment described here is expensive, and much of it can be purchased from any fine kitchen store or restaurant supply store or online. A few things may seem nonessential, like a good funnel. But when you've spilled half an infusion that took you four weeks to make because you had a piddly little two-inch funnel, you might feel differently about springing the $10 for a nice one.

The recipes are not difficult. If you can brew a cup of tea and make your own salad dressing, you can tackle anything within these pages. Many of the recipes revolve around prep—lightly crushing spices first instead of just tossing them in the mix, or finely slicing citrus rind to capture every last bit of its essential oils—and patience is the number one skill needed. Some of the equipment might just become a staple in your kitchen, like the mortar and pestle.

Here is a list of equipment needed for making the majority of recipes, followed by a list of basic bar equipment and a little chart about measurements explaining my annoying practice of using ounces and cups.

BASIC EQUIPMENT

Measuring cups & spoons, bowls, a pitcher or two

You need at least one set of measuring cups and spoons and at least one large measuring pitcher. A few additional glass pitchers, jars, and bowls—to hold infusions, spices, ingredients, and things you are straining—will make everything easier for you.

Microplane rasp

Picture a small cheese grater with a handle and the thinnest holes. A microplaner helps you follow your bliss in the kitchen, opening doors where there were only walls, to misquote Joseph Campbell. How did you ever grate ginger before you owned one? Did you, even? How did cheese get on your pasta? Lemon zest in your everything? This $15 tool makes removing the zest from limes and oranges incredibly simple and fast. It gets all the aromatic skin with none of the pith. When grating ginger, the microplaner breaks up the fibers within the root beautifully, creating something almost like a purée.

Mortar & pestle

If you do not already own this ancient two-piece implement, you will need one to assist you in liberating the good juju from seeds and spices. You will then know the small zen of grinding your own spice, a kind of satisfaction no pepper mill can deliver.

Coffee grinder, co-opted

If the romance of the mortar and pestle escapes you, an extra coffee grinder can pinch hit to break down and grind spices. You can pulse them as you would coffee to fully grind a spice, or give a few pulses just to access the volatiles. You'll want to give it a thorough wipe down between uses so oils don't comingle.

Heavy-bottomed saucepans

A two-quart saucepan is needed to heat and steep simple syrups in any quantity and to make certain tinctures. One saucepan should take care of most recipes except those of large quantity (like larger volumes of vermouth). The heavy bottom is essential when using sugars and fruit so you don't scorch or burn the ingredients.

Disposable tea bags
Use disposable tea bags when making infusions with several spices; for pulling out certain ingredients that infuse faster and may over-power, like hibiscus or the very bitter gentian root; and especially when using any ingredient of which you are unsure. Tea bags also can help make infusions and tinctures clearer and easier to finish (less intensive straining). Any tea shop or Asian specialty grocery will carry disposable tea bags in packs of 100.

Funnel
A funnel should be large enough to fit your mesh strainer within its top or easily handle a few layers of cheesecloth. You can get a 5- or 6-inch funnel with detachable strainer to separate solids more easily and speed up double straining for $10 to $15 at any better kitchen store.

Handheld mesh strainer
Made of fine or double-fine mesh, this tool will be the cleanest way to strain and fine your infusions. Strainers come in many sizes. You want one about the size of half a medium orange—small enough to use when straining drinks—and another that nests within a funnel when making infusions. These strainers live in better kitchen stores and restaurant supply shops.

Cheesecloth
Also for straining, cheesecloth especially helps when you want to squeeze liquid out of macerated fruit. You want to use two or three layers depending upon what you're trying to strain. Find in any gro-cery store, usually near the last-minute cooking implement section next to the disposable roasting pans.

Coffee filters
For the finest in fining, line your strainer or funnel with a coffee fil-ter, preferably unbleached. If you have a good deal of particulate in your infusion, you might have to change filters, which will take a little

longer. To make clearer bitters or infusions, they are worth the time. If you're a coffee person, you can use your French press as a strainer.

Bottles & jars

You'll need a variety of bottles, jars, and containers for storing your concoctions, but many can be recycled from what you already have in your kitchen.

Use recycled wine or liquor bottles to store your finished products, but use wide-mouth jars to cut down on time dealing with all the things you'll be using to infuse, like zest, star anise, and herbs. Kerr and Ball are the most common brands, and they are cheapest when purchased by the case. Your friendly neighborhood Ace hardware store is always a good bet for its variety of stock on hand.

One-cup canning jars: If you decide to go off the deep end, these small jars will allow you to macerate herbs and spices separately, creating an army of tinctures with which to blend custom bitters according to your every whim. Ninety-nine percent of you will never care this much, but for the one percent, kudos.

One-pint canning jars: Many recipes for bitters yield one pint—16 ounces or 2 cups.

One-quart canning jars: When a recipe calls for 3 cups of spirit, which is basically the equivalent of 1 bottle (750ml), it usually has no more than 1 cup of simple syrup or other addition of liquid, which makes these 1-quart or 4-cup jars perfect for infusions.

Pickle jars, the 1-gallon type you see at stores selling quantities of foodstuffs and condiments in megasizes, come in handy when making sangria or ginger ale, serving punch, or making a large batch of infusion for gifts.

Save wine and beer bottles and buy new corks and stoppers for them. Liquor and wine bottles with screw caps work even better, as do those with porcelain or plastic latches. Recycled condiment jars and small canning jars work for adjuncts and things made in smaller batches. Always make sure your bottles are clean and sterilized before use.

To store your wares in something stylish or to gift them, check out your local kitchen store, Cost Plus, or an online site like Specialty

Bottle (www.specialtybottle.com). Here you can find very cool amber bottles in sizes small enough for bitters, say 4 ounces, and also purchase caps to add to them for dashing, like those you see on top of hot sauce bottles, as well as bottles with eyedroppers.

A NOTE ABOUT STERILIZING . . .

Don't worry, we're not canning. But these recipes are chock-full of organic materials and sometimes sugar, so you want to inhibit the growth of . . . stuff as much as you can. That's why most recipes with sugar and those with lower alcohol ask you to bring things to a boil for a little while. Sterilizing the jars and bottles you use, even though you are combining things with high-proof alcohol, is just the right thing to do.

Safety first, in two easy steps. To start, make sure the lid or lid pieces go with the jar so you can achieve an airtight seal. If you are using canning jars, check that the rubber seals of the lids are still intact.

1. Wash the jars and bottles you are to use as if you have a temporary case of OCD. Use a bottle brush or a toothbrush. Nooks and crannies, nooks and crannies . . .

2. Sterilize the lids and bottles and any removable tops or caps by submerging them in boiling water for 15 minutes. It's a good idea to sterilize right before using them.

3. Let all dry.

BAR EQUIPMENT

For making drinks at home, you really need only a few basic tools; everything else is just a gadget. Get multiples of each if you like to throw parties so you can make more than one drink at a time. You can find many kinds in kitchen stores, but they're a bit cheaper at restaurant supply stores for the bare-bones generic versions.

Tins & mixing glasses

Some cocktails need to be shaken. Of course, you can shake any cocktail you like—James Bond would approve. Using a metal tin—a thin container that is slightly bigger and taller than a pint glass—and mixing glass (a pint glass) in conjunction with a strainer  makes the process as simple as possible, as opposed to the tins that have a little top and a hat. The colander-size holes in their tops let chunks of ice through, and sometimes the chill of the drink causes them to stick together.

Bar spoon

Better to mix with, but any spoonlike thing with a long handle will suffice.

Measuring equipment for ounces

These can be standard jiggers, which are small, metal, and double-coned and come in a few combinations of sizes. Get one that has a 1½-ounce big side and another that has a 2-ounce big side. You can also find small fluid-ounce measuring cups for up to 2 or 3 ounces, with every half-ounce measure noted. These are handy for less spillage and are much better for home use. You can measure out the base spirit, transfer it to your mixing glass, and then typically have enough room to mix the rest of all the cocktail ingredients.

Hawthorne strainer

You put this strainer over the mixing glass for straining into its final destination. It grabs most ice chunks and does the job for 95 percent of cocktails.

Smaller fine-mesh strainer

These come in handy for many things in the kitchen—sifting and hand squeezing citrus in addition to straining. In the bar this strainer catches small chips of ice and bigger bits of flotsam when you want a clearer or less chunky beverage. It also comes in handy when transferring infusions.

AND NOW, A THING ABOUT MEASUREMENTS . . .

In this book, drink recipes are measured in ounces because that's how cocktails are made. Infusions, bitters, and batch recipes use the units of measurement most common in cooking—cups and spoons—because that's what is used in the home.

Here's a handy conversion chart for measurements:

½ fluid ounce = 3 teaspoons

1 tablespoon = 3 teaspoons

1 fluid ounce = 2 tablespoons

1½ fluid ounces = 3 tablespoons (standard bar serving of liquor)

¼ cup = 4 tablespoons

1 cup = 8 fluid ounces

1 cup = 16 tablespoons

1 pint = 16 fluid ounces

1 fifth = 25.36 fluid ounces

1 fifth = 750ml (standard wine/liquor bottle)

Vague units of measure often used in bar books:

1 dash = 6 drops

1 dram – ¾ teaspoon (4 drams per tablespoon)

1 pony = 1 ounce

1 jigger = depends on the jigger

A note on measurements: Spices and herbs are sold by the ounce, as a unit of weight. The spice list in this book (page 8) includes the rough conversion rate from this measurement to cooking measurements, so you know how much of an herb or spice you need to buy. If something you want is not listed, find something like it to compare weight.

~ Liquors, Preferably ~

Rather than litter every recipe with my suggestions for certain alcohols and brands, I thought I'd just get it out of the way in one short burst of Nascar decal–inspired shameless promotion.

You can use whatever spirits you like to make your infusions and bitters, but this is what I use based on what's cheapest in my state. After bartending for more than fifteen years, I'll own my opinions, but I will not argue them.

My rule follows the pearls-before-swine theory. If it's that god-awful when you drink it straight, don't waste more money or high-quality herbs or fruit on trying to dress it up. Rot gut is as rot gut does, in other words. I recommend the following liquors only if I'd put them in the well of my bar. If they're not good enough to hang in a simple "and soda" or "and tonic," I don't touch them.

If you can't find one of the brands listed here at your local liquor store, ask your retailer for something comparable in price and quality.

VODKA

I really never want to have another discussion ever again about what vodka is better or best. Because you are all wrong. The point is moot. Moot! Vodka, by its very ass-kicking nature, is supposed to be odorless, colorless, and tasteless. Therefore, whatever tastes clean enough to you is best. Bottom-shelf vodka tastes like crap because of impurities, from lazy or little filtering, not from any lack of technique. Your tall, frosty bottle on the top shelf is 750 milliliters of naked emperor. Get something in the middle. What you can afford. Subject closed.

Gordon's is the cheapest, cleanest 80-proof vodka for infusing. Depending upon sale price, I also recommend Smirnoff and Monopolowa. I also fly the Seattle flag with Batch 206, but you might not be able to get it where you reside.

For faster infusions or more intense extractions, use higher-proof (over 100) vodka. Smirnoff and Stoli both make a higher proof. Also, there is Everclear—clocking in at 190 proof, but that's a bit extreme. You will need to dilute these infusions to make them palatable and to keep from KOing unwitting guinea pigs and yourself.

GIN

See the above statement on vodka and consider how this can affect gin as well. Choosing a gin for your cocktail or one with which to infuse hinges upon your flavor preferences. If you're infusing a gin, you probably want to start with something that has a basic, balanced character. Beefeater gin is not only the gin I recommend for infusions, it's also what comprises my martinis. It has perfect balance and textbook aromatics, with no one note dominating the mix.

WHISK(E)Y

Depending upon from whence it came, the word does or does not contain an *e*. I don't rely on just one brown, so I'll recommend one or two from each of the following categories: rye/dry, bourbon, and Scotch. I spend a little more on the brown liquors I use.

Rye/dry: Use a rye or dry whiskey when you don't want to impart as much sweetness from wood in your infusion. Rittenhouse 100-proof rye definitely sticks its head above the pack for value, and the flavor is clean and fairly dry. Jim Beam Yellow Label rye is another contender, if you can find it. I'm also a sucker for Jameson Irish on sale.

Bourbon: Use bourbon in an infusion when you want to bring in those telltale notes of new oak, all vanilla sweetness, and warm spice. I recommend Jim Beam Black Label 8 year for its superior smoothness and flavor at the price point. George Dickel No. 12 is also a great bet, and less sweet. If I can get it on sale, I will always bow toward Maker's Mark.

SCOTCH

Obviously, we're talking about a blended whiskey here, due to cost, but you use Scotch in an infusion when you want to pass on some earth, smoke, or peat—no reason otherwise. I wouldn't go below Dewar's in this category, and my personal favorite is Famous Grouse.

RUM

If you want to use white (clear) rum, *don't*. Cheap white rum is no one's friend. You're better off for the money finding an affordable *cachaça*. I will say no more. Appleton Estate is the oldest distillery in Jamaica, and I use their entry-level rum in my wells and for all my infusions because it is lighter dark rum, with an average age of more than five years. Nothing beats it for the price, but I have never spent much time thinking about rum. If you want something with less barrel-aged flavor, try Lemon Hart 80 proof or Gosling's.

BRANDY

This category sucks because the cheap stuff is often not nearly as good as whiskeys costing many dollars less. Yeah, yeah, brandy is distilled from wine, and whiskey is distilled basically from beer—fruit and grain, totally different. But if you can't tell the difference, what's the difference? I don't know. I look for Martell VS or St. Remy VSOP, and I don't look back.

TEQUILA

I can't skimp on tequila, and neither should you. I love it so much. Throughout my career I have relied on Sauza Hornitos, a *reposado*, as my go-to in a margarita and an infusion. *Reposado* refers to the most basic requirements for resting and aging tequila. It has always packed the truest flavor for the least money. I also like El Jimador Reposado Tequila, mainly because nothing is ever on sale in my state. If you've got the cash, and it's on sale, go for Cazadores reposado. (Their white is the lowest I'll spend for white—unaged—tequila.)

The following liquors will come less into play, so I'll rattle them off:

CACHAÇA

Ypioca or Pitu are the most common brands in the liquor store as well as the ones with the best flavor and lowest hangover factor.

PISCO

Most readily available in major metropolitan areas, Alto del Carmen pisco has the aroma you want a grape brandy to possess—like inhaling the very kernel of the grape. I much prefer it to cheap grappa. Hell, you can call it grappa if you want to. Great pisco is all about nuance when you're featuring it solo, but that gets lost fast when you're infusing; so save the good stuff for sipping.

Infusions: Liquors,
∼ Liqueurs & Tinctures ∼

More than a decade ago, infused vodka and candy shop–worthy *-tinis* (as in *martinis*) were all the rage, and bars not in hotels that specialized in classic cocktails existed in pockets—the alcoholic refuge, the "-tini resistance." Nowadays, bartenders verging on cosplay—with their pork pie hats and arm garters—and well read in cocktail lore are helping turn the tide toward historically inspired, spirituous cocktails (read: all booze), relying less on sweet and more on bitter and sour. As are the tides, so are the cocktails, and our lives.

Whether you're a serious cocktail nerd or just doing it for the novelty, it all goes back to putting some things in a jar with booze, and waiting. The recipes in this book take into account that not everyone likes to be confronted with myriad herbs in an *amaro* or esoteric gin. Some of us just want a cold, refreshing drink that requires zero analysis, and there exists great middle ground between the Appletini and a Fernet Manhattan.

Knowing what makes your cocktail taste the way it does helps you decide how you want to tinker with it, and this book has only one rule: Drinking is an adult pastime. Stuff with booze in it should taste like booze is in it.

TYPES OF INFUSIONS

What exactly you make is determined by a few factors that break down into three basic categories: liquor, liqueur, and tincture. The definitions of these three liquids are malleable, but for the purposes of this book, think about the intensity of an infusion and how you might use it—as a main ingredient or as a complement.

Liquor

Technically, a liquor is an alcoholic beverage that has been distilled rather than fermented. Liquor can have flavor added from botanicals (gin), wood (whiskey), fruit, and spice. In practice, think of a liquor as the base in a cocktail recipe—rum, vodka, gin, whiskey, and brandy. It can be a little sweet, and many liquors ride the line between this world and the next—ouzo and akvavit, for example. Eighty proof (40 percent alcohol by volume) is the most common strength of a liquor.

Liqueur

A liqueur, or cordial, is sweetened liquor that can begin life as anything from vodka to brandy and has additional sugar and flavoring from botanicals, nuts, fruits, and more. Sometimes liqueurs have a lower percentage of alcohol than a liquor has, for many around 40 to 50 proof (20 to 25 percent alcohol by volume). Some liqueurs are proprietary recipes sold and recognized by brand name, such as Chartreuse or Drambuie, and they have unique flavor profiles based on a variety of ingredients. (Anything on the shelf with a name straight out of a text message or top billing at a strip club fits this category, too—e.g., Hpnotiq.) Other liqueurs fall into certain categories, such as anisettes or triple secs or anything that starts with "crème de," and they are expressions of a certain flavor, say of orange or spice or berry. Whether based on fruits, nuts, or a variety of herbs and spices, a liqueur is the Cointreau in your margarita, literally. It's the ½- to ¾-ounce ingredient in a cocktail that makes the entire thing sing.

Tinctures

Think of the little vials of remedies you see in the health food store. A tincture is a very concentrated infusion, usually with a dominant herb or spice, or, in health uses, a dominant purpose. Technically, a tincture is anything stored in alcohol or another solvent for preservation. Use tinctures by the dropperful because they are too strong in flavor. Bitters are tinctures. If you want to avoid over-bittering, you can always make a tincture of single bittering agents to be blended together. That's 200-level stuff to think about when and if you get bit by the bitters bug.

TO INFUSE, MACERATE, OR STEEP?

To infuse something means to soak in liquid without boiling in order to extract desirable compounds. When you steep something, you are infusing in a heated or boiling solution, like when you make tea. Macerating is the same as steeping, but it does not take into account the temperature of the solution first. To macerate also refers to the breaking down or softening of something, an appropriate term when using fresh fruit or produce. In this book steeping refers to the process of infusing with heat, and macerating refers to the process of infusing without heat.

Call it an infusion or an extraction. Infusion is the alcohol-centric word; extraction is the science lab, ingredient-centric word, though we commonly associate an extract with something highly concentrated and potent, as in vanilla extract.

INGREDIENTS

Always procure the highest quality ingredients you can, to the point that it makes sense. For example, Madagascar vanilla beans make a big difference in a delicate flan, but when you're dumping them in 80-proof booze, the lesser expensive Mexican vanilla beans will work just as well and cost half as much.

The fresher the better, and organic whenever possible. You are leeching volatile compounds out of whatever you are infusing, which may include the compound that gives anise its telltale flavor (*anethole*) or a pesticide. Alcohol doesn't know the difference; so know from whence your ingredients came.

Whole spices will help maintain the liquid's clarity, but lightly crushing them in a mortar and pestle helps release their volatiles and can speed the infusing process. Toasting the spices can alter and enhance the flavor, especially the seeds—dill, fennel, or caraway.

WHY DOES MY LIQUEUR OR BITTERS TASTE DIFFERENT?

You'll notice that many of your infusions and liqueurs just don't have quite the mouthfeel of some commercially made products; it has something to do with how they sweeten the liqueur, commercially. Mouthfeel refers to the way in which a liquid reacts to your palate upon entry, around the tongue and on the gums, on through until after you swallow. Think about how different it is to sip and swallow a mouthful of half and half as opposed to skim milk. The former has more weight to it and coats the mouth. A liqueur, because of sugar content, coats the mouth as well. Many liqueurs also contain glycerin, which is used in both food and beauty products. It also can be found—though not listed—in many wines for improved mouthfeel. Though not necessarily bad for you, glycerin doesn't exactly fit the mind-set of this book. I register my ambivalence. If you want a thicker, heavier mouthfeel without adding sweetness, you can find food-grade glycerin where you buy homebrew supplies.

To naturally boost the mouthfeel of some liqueurs, keep them in the freezer. If you like the increased unctuousness of vodka out of the icebox, you can achieve that in an akvavit by substituting Invert Sugar Syrup (page 48), which provides a weightier mouthfeel.

Adjuncts: Bitters,
⌁ Syrups, Salts & Sugars ⌁

Layering is a common enough concept in the kitchen, in making perfume, in music. Even in the beauty that is ice-cold gin in a glass, in this seemingly one perfect thing different botanicals merge in harmony to make it so. In the margarita, sweet plays with sour accented by salt and the slight bitterness of tequila and lime rind for what may possibly be the greatest cocktail in the world. Of all drinks, those that play with multiple tastes—sweet, sour, salty, bitter—hold the most sway and make the major impressions.

Playing with these four flavors, and the way you add them to a drink, can elevate even the most basic highball, whether it's rhubarb bitters in your whiskey soda or a bit of spicy salt added to a rum sour. Think of what's in the glass in the same way you would think of something on a plate or in a bowl. What does the drink need? If it's too sweet, add a squeeze of citrus or, as you'll learn, a little vinegar. If it's too sour, add a little sweet.

In the bar arsenal, the following ingredients act as condiments, going in, on top of, or, literally, on the side of your drink. Just like a well-stocked pantry, having some of these happy little substances in the refrigerator and on your wet bar can open a host of possibilities in even the easiest of drinks.

Let's get back to the salad dressing metaphor one more time for reinforcement. Simple balsamic vinaigrette will contain oil, vinegar, a little mustard, and a squeeze of honey—savory, sour, bitter, and sweet.

When you make salad dressing, you add more of some and a little of each until it's the right consistency and taste for you. Drinks are just like that, but instead you work from an accepted template and add an extra half bar spoon of simple syrup, a few more drops at a time of bitters, a splash of citrus juice or vinegar to tweak it to your taste.

The recipe for any cocktail is a guideline bartenders follow to the letter to produce consistent results. The only result you're looking for is the one that makes you happiest and master of your DIY universe.

The following recipes are ways to provide the sweet, salty, bitter, and sour in your drinks.

ᴥ Simple Syrup ᴥ

More than making drinks sweet, sugar tames the hot feeling of alcohol on the tongue and adds a richer feel to a drink, especially one served without ice. Sugar is the reason the average liqueur tastes thicker than the average liquor. Margaritas made from scratch depend on it to tame the sour component, just like a touch of honey in salad dressing rounds out the vinegar.

Granulated sugar does not dissolve in a cold drink or alcohol. Simple syrup involves dissolving granulated sugar in hot water and then cooling the solution for use in drinks from iced tea to a sidecar. Make simple syrup in larger batches and keep a jar in the refrigerator.

Makes 1 cup

1 cup water
1 cup sugar

Bring water to a boil and stir in the sugar until it dissolves completely. Remove from the heat and let cool.

Transfer to a sterilized glass jar or bottle with an airtight lid. Keep refrigerated and use as needed.

The ratio for this recipe is always 1:1, whether you're making half a cup in the microwave or a large batch for a party. If you prefer your drinks less sweet, however, you can change the recipe to as little as ½ cup sugar for 1 cup water.

BROWN SUGAR SIMPLE SYRUP

Change the flavor by using other sugars. Using the above Simple Syrup recipe, substitute 1 cup turbinado or brown sugar (light or dark) for regular sugar. The darker the brown sugar, the more the flavor will change, becoming richer or more intense.

HONEY SYRUP

Honey has the potential to add a great deal of character to an otherwise simple syrup. Consider that when using it and taste your honey first.

Follow the directions in the recipe for Simple Syrup, using ¾ cup honey (instead of sugar) for every 1 cup water. Try using a fragrant honey, from lavender or other flowers, to complement certain drinks of your choice.

INVERT SUGAR SYRUP

When you heat simple syrup with acid, the sucrose breaks into glucose and fructose (all are kinds of sugar). The term *inverted* refers to the differing properties between the sugars, but don't worry your pretty little head about that. By inverting the sugar, you obtain a simple syrup with a softer taste. The fast-fading sweetness enhances the fruity or spicy characteristics of what you taste, allegedly. (It's true.)

To the Simple Syrup recipe, add ¼ teaspoon of citric or tartaric acid to the water before boiling. You can also use 1 tablespoon lemon juice. Follow the rest of the recipe.

⌒ **Flavored Simple Syrup** ⌒

Flavored simple syrup is the easiest way to alter a drink. Think of how herbs and spices are used together in food and in cocktails, and let that begin the storm in your brain for adulterating simple syrup as well as the other add-ons in this chapter. Lemon syrup can easily become lemon ginger syrup, likewise mint into mint-lime for a cheater on the Mojito (page 182).

Use the Simple Syrup recipe for all the following variations—and note their variations, too.

HERBAL SYRUP

This recipe uses mint, but you can substitute for whatever you like: rosemary, sage, tarragon, etc. Many varieties of mint exist. You want something that has more than just the hallmark peppermint extract note. I have the best luck at the farmers' market. In a perfect world, you'd grow your own in a pot on your porch or an entire bed in your backyard—easy enough since mint behaves like a weed.

Makes about 1 cup

½ cup additional water
1 cup fresh mint plus additional, roughly chopped

If you really want to coax out the oils, first bruise the mint with a little sugar in the mortar and pestle to rough it up a little.

Follow the Simple Syrup directions, adding the extra water.

Add the mint after the sugar is dissolved and reduce the heat to the lowest setting.

Let the mixture steep for 30 minutes; remove from the heat and let sit for a few hours. Strain into a sterilized, airtight jar and refrigerate.

CITRUS SYRUP

Makes about 1 cup

1 cup additional water
Zest of three lemons
A favorite herb or spice (optional)

Follow the Simple Syrup directions, adding the water, zest, and herb or spice before bringing the water to a boil.

After adding the sugar, reduce to the lowest heat and simmer until the volume is reduced by half.

Remove from the heat, strain and store in a sterilized, airtight jar.

VARIATIONS:

- Add 1 tablespoon of lightly crushed coriander seeds to make a Lemon Coriander Syrup.

SPICE SYRUP

Makes about 1 cup

1 cup additional water
1 tablespoon lightly crushed spice: cardamom, grains of paradise, anise seed, etc.
3 cinnamon sticks, broken
Zest of 1 lemon or orange

Follow the Simple Syrup directions, adding the water, cardamom, cinnamon sticks, and zest to the simple syrup water in a saucepan; combine and bring to a boil. Stir in the sugar until it dissolves completely.

Remove from the heat and let cool. Transfer to a glass jar or bottle with tight-fitting lid. Keep the spice and zest in the syrup for up to 1 week, checking for flavor. When ready, strain the mixture into a sterilized, airtight jar. Keep refrigerated and use as needed.

- After 1 week in the syrup, the zest will be candied. You can use it as a garnish in drinks or on desserts (see page 68).

GINGER SYRUP

Makes about 1 cup

1 cup additional water
¼ cup minced fresh gingerroot

Follow the Simple Syrup directions, adding the water and ginger before bringing to a boil. After adding the sugar, reduce to the lowest heat and simmer until the volume reduces by half.

Remove from the heat and store in a jar overnight or up to 3 days before straining. After the syrup is strained, refrigerate in a sterilized, airtight jar.

LAVENDER SYRUP

Makes about 1 cup

2 tablespoons lavender
½ cup additional water 2 tablespoons lavender

Add the lavender before bringing the water to a boil.

Follow the Simple Syrup directions, adding the extra water.

Allow the syrup to cool, then strain into a sterilized, airtight jar and refrigerate.

VARIATIONS:

- For the lavender, substitute one of the following: ⅓ cup hyssop, ½ cup jasmine, ⅓ cup rosebuds.

SAGE SYRUP

Makes about 1 cup

⅓ cup fresh sage leaves
½ cup additional water

Bruise the sage in a mortar and pestle with a little bit of sugar.

Follow the Simple Syrup directions, adding the sage leaves and water before boiling. Allow the syrup to cool, then strain into a sterilized, airtight jar and refrigerate.

—————

VARIATIONS:

• Substitute lemon verbena, thyme, or sweet marjoram for the sage.

ᴗ **Homemade Sugar Cubes** ᴗ

Homemade sugar cubes seem a little artsy-craftsy, but you'll never make an easier or cheaper present (to accompany a bottle of bubbles). They're also a quick fix to dress up a cheap bubbly, and make a wonderful start to a julep if you sub a mint tincture. Use candy molds or tiny cookie cutters for shapes, if you'd like to go that far.

Makes 4 dozen ½-inch cubes

4 teaspoons your favorite bitters
1½ cups white sugar

Mix the bitters into the sugar a little at a time. When all is said and done, the mixture will feel a little damp, like the sand just under the surface at the beach. Add more sugar if it's too wet, more liquid if it's too dry.

Pour the sugar onto a parchment or wax paper–lined cookie sheet. Press it into a long rectangle until it's nice and compact and as tall as you want your cubes, rectangles, or rhombuses to be (shape is your business).

Using a pastry cutter or long knife, cut into ½-inch strips, then carefully cut those strips into cubes. Let sit for 15 minutes.

Preheat the oven to 150 degrees F. With a knife, gently separate the cubes. Place the cookie sheet in the oven for 15 minutes to strengthen and harden

---

VARIATIONS:

- For extra-sturdy sugar cubes, mix 2 teaspoons powdered egg white with the wet ingredient before adding to the sugar.

- Keep on hand to add to glasses of bubbly for an instant champagne cocktail, or give a bag of them as a gift with a bottle of prosecco.

⋏ Finishing Sugar ⋏

Just as you can infuse salt with flavor, so can you infuse sugar. Use finishing sugar in a drink that calls for muddling with fruit or mint or for decorating the rim of the glass—but just half the rim; this isn't 1997. You can also dust the top of a drink with it, as was the practice in merrie olde England. I keep an extra coffee grinder just for spices, which also makes most of the following recipes easier. Granulated sugar is OK to use, but superfine is, well, it's all in the name.

LIME SUGAR

This sugar adds extra fragrance, nuance, and snap to any drink where citrus is a key component. A sugar rim is the finishing touch on a Sidecar (page 179). You may use any citrus you like.

Makes ¼ cup

6 medium limes, finely zested
1 teaspoon kosher salt
3½ tablespoons sugar, divided

Preheat the oven to 100 degrees F and line a baking sheet with foil. Don't use parchment paper because it might absorb some of the oil you want for the sugar.

Combine the zest with the salt and 1 tablespoon of the sugar; spread on the prepared baking sheet and bake for 30 minutes. Allow the mixture to cool; grind in a spice grinder until very fine.

Combine with the remaining 2½ tablespoons of sugar and store in an airtight jar.

MINT SUGAR

This sugar can adorn any tart beach drink (beach not required), but really shines as the garnish for a highball, such as Bitter Lemon Soda (page 176).

Makes ¼ cup

½ cup mint leaves, cleaned and dried
4 tablespoons sugar, divided

Preheat the oven to 100 degrees F and line a baking sheet with foil. Don't use parchment because it might absorb some of the oil you want for the sugar.

Finely chop the mint leaves and mix with 1 tablespoon of the sugar. Put on the prepared baking sheet and bake for 30 minutes. Allow the mixture to cool; grind in a spice grinder until very fine.

Combine with the remaining 3 tablespoons of sugar and store in an airtight jar.

CARDAMOM SUGAR

You probably made cinnamon sugar all the time as a kid. Same with cardamom; get the freshest ground cardamom you can buy or—ideally—grind it yourself.

Makes ¼ cup

3 tablespoons sugar
1½ tablespoons ground cardamom

Combine the sugar and cardamom; store in an airtight jar.

FLAVORED SUGAR (USING TINCTURE)

Don't worry about getting sugar wet, as long as you do it a little bit at a time. Bakeries do this all the time for "sanding sugar," and it's how you get colored sugar for cookies and cupcakes. In this case, you're going for flavor instead of color.

Makes ¼ cup

¼ cup sugar
1 teaspoon bitters or herb or spice tincture

Place the sugar in a small bowl. Add the bitters 1 drizzle at a time, using a fork to stir the mixture thoroughly in between additions. Store in an airtight jar.

GINGER SUGAR

In 1800s England when ginger brew and ale were the rage, barkeeps sprinkled the tops of drinks with ginger sugar. Ginger was as widely available as pepper and was seen as an affordable luxury of the not-so-Dickensian.

Makes ¼ cup

1 tablespoon fresh gingerroot
¼ cup sugar

Preheat the oven to 100 degrees F and line a baking sheet with foil. (Parchment paper would absorb some of the precious zing.)

Rasp the gingerroot so the bits are superfine. Mix a little at a time with the sugar.

Place on the prepared baking sheet and bake for 15 minutes. Allow the mixture to cool.

Grind in a spice grinder until fine. Store in an airtight jar.

⌁ Finishing Salt ⌁

You eat food; therefore you know what salt can do. Salt draws out flavor, or rather filters out certain flavors, ergo, enhancing other flavors. It's science. The most common use for salt in cocktails is on the rim of a glass containing a margarita. My favorite use is for the chile-lime mix I use on the rim of a Perro Salado (page 162), a Salty Dog (vodka and grapefruit) made with tequila.

CITRUS SALT

The margarita exemplifies the perfect use of a salt rim, therefore using salt boosted with lime is even more perfect. The Sidecar (page 179) and citrus sugar is the yang to this yin. Try blending the two in different proportions and see what happens.

Makes ¼ cup

3½ tablespoons coarse sea salt
3 tablespoons (5 to 6 limes) fresh lime zest, or your favorite citrus

Preheat the oven to 100 degrees F and line a baking sheet with foil. Don't use parchment paper because it might absorb some of the oil you want in the salt.

Make a pile of the salt on the prepared baking sheet and place the zest on top. Bake for 30 minutes. Allow the mixture to cool.

Separate the zest (some salt is fine) and grind in a spice grinder until fine. Combine with the salt and store in an airtight jar.

VARIATIONS:

- Add 2 teaspoons freshly ground chile powder (medium spicy or to taste), or 1 teaspoon sugar, or both.

- Substitute citrus at will.

CELERY SALT

A salty rim on a Bloody Mary might be a little much for many, but those many are wrong.

Makes ¼ cup

2 teaspoons celery seed
1 teaspoon fennel seed
3 tablespoons kosher salt

Grind the celery seed and fennel seed together in a grinder; add the salt and pulse once or twice. This move not only helps clean the grinder, but it also allows the salt to pick up some oil from the seeds. Store in an airtight jar.

VARIATIONS:

- Use caraway seeds if you like to start your Bloody Mary with akvavit instead of vodka, and use cumin if you like a Bloody Maria (tequila).

SPICED SALT

A little salt improves ice cream, chocolate desserts, and so much more. To add oomph, I like a dash of spiced salt in my sours. You might not. Look at it this way: you'll ruin only one drink and you can use the rest of the stuff in rum balls.

Makes ¼ cup

1 teaspoon cardamom
1 teaspoon grains of paradise
3½ tablespoons kosher salt

Grind the cardamom and grains of paradise together in a grinder; add the salt and pulse once or twice. This move not only helps clean the grinder, but it also allows the salt to pick up some oil from the seeds. Store in an airtight jar.

VARIATIONS:

- Replace spices with any of the following combos: hibiscus and cinnamon; fennel and juniper berries; vanilla and a miniscule amount of lavender; nigella seed and rosebuds.

∽ Bitterness ∾

Cocktail bitters evolved from tinctures, which were originally used for medicinal purposes until someone discovered they added extra enjoyment to the after-work tonic of choice.

The biggest problem with making bitters at home is the rate at which herbs, spices, and fruit give up their essence: they're all different. It'd be easier to dump all of them into a jar with booze and forget about it for a few weeks, but some ingredients would overpower the mix. The cloying note of lavender can ruin anything drinkable or edible, and fennel seed can turn an infusion into low-grade ouzo right quick.

Using disposable tea bags or tea balls (little perforated metal cages that hold tea and act in place of a tea bag) or separating the ingredients to begin with all help moderate the results. I wrote each recipe to get it to a relatively foolproof place, but you can always go further toward mad scientist and make tinctures for each bittering agent and some spices and blend them yourself, like a perfumer. That's how I do it, but that seemed . . . excessive. Alternatively, if a recipe requires only two weeks for the bittering agents, you can add them in at the end as opposed to the beginning—whatever is simpler.

Each bitters has three components: A. What makes it bitter; B. What gives it flavor; C. What is the base. Normally, I add a touch of sweetener to smooth the raspy edges and add body, either molasses or a syrup.

BASIC BITTERS

Using the A, B, and C components, here is a plug-and-play recipe to make your own bitters. At first keep the bittering agents to a minimum because there is such a thing as too much. When you are more comfortable with what packs what kind of wallop, you can better adjust to your taste. You can use whatever liquor you like, but a lower proof (80 proof, the most common) might need more time to macerate.

Makes 1½ cups

BASE:

1 cup high-proof vodka (100-proof or higher)

FLAVORINGS:

6 juniper berries

1 star anise

Zest of 1 lemon

BITTERING AGENTS:

½ teaspoon gentian root

½ teaspoon horehound

In a sterilized jar, combine the vodka with the juniper, star anise, and zest. Let the mixture macerate for 2 weeks, shaking daily.

Add the gentian root and horehound. Macerate for 1 week, again shaking daily.

Strain the entire mixture to remove as much herb and spice as possible, and then strain it again with a coffee filter to remove all the bitter flotsam. Store in a sterilized airtight jar at room temperature.

Time is the biggest factor in making bitters. Think about the ingredients as a function of time. For example, rosemary and lavender are very pungent and distinct, and you don't want them in an infusion for as long as you might want lemon zest. Add extra pungent spice at the same time as the bittering agents, or later.

VARIATIONS:

- Experiment with different bittering agents:

    —Strong and silent choices (i.e., little aroma or flavor added) include angostura, gentian root, and myrrh.

    —Medium to mild and aromatic choices include bitter orange peel, chamomile, coriander, dandelion, goldenseal, hibiscus, hops, mugwort, tea, wormwood, and yarrow root.

↷ Drinking Vinegar ↶

There's an old Taoist parable called "The Vinegar Tasters" that also has a recurring, corresponding illustration of three men surrounding a barrel of vinegar. The men are said to represent the main religious and philosophical traditions of China: Confucianism, Buddhism, and Taoism (Confucius, Buddha, and Lao Zi).

Each man's expression shows his reaction to the vinegar and thus his outlook on life. Confucius's face is puckered; he sees life as sour and in need of rules and guidelines. Buddha looks stern; he sees life in terms of pain and suffering, hence the bitter expression. Lao Zi is all smiles; he believes all living things are intrinsically good. He tastes the vinegar without judging it.

This has nothing and everything to do with drinking vinegar. The naturally sour and aromatic notes of vinegar mixed with simple syrup and maybe a fruit for flavor make every taste bud stand at attention, ready for action, salivating for food. Since hunting for vinegar drinks or making syrups from things like tamarind or sour-plum paste might not fit into everyone's schedule, I recommend you start simply with apple cider vinegar to see if this type of drink is for you. (If not, you've got something with which to make salad dressing.) Try a few teaspoons in a glass of soda water to check your level of enthusiasm. Vinegar tonics have a long tradition in folk medicine, used as a detoxifier, digestion aid, and immune-system booster. None of these claims is scientifically proven, blah, blah, blah...

You can hunt out exotic vinegars, but use organic rice wine vinegar or apple cider vinegar as a base for all the recipes that follow. The former provides a blanker canvas and softer sour; the latter curls your toes.

PLAIN DRINKING VINEGAR

Working on the same principle as a basic vinaigrette recipe, use this recipe as a template and adjust to your taste. If I use apple cider vinegar, for example, I bump up the sugar slightly, since I perceive apple cider vinegar as extra sour. Motherly note: sugars and organic matter—even in vinegar—can be a breeding ground for bad bacteria, so please refrigerate any vinegar you've tinkered with.

Makes 1 cup

⅔ cup light vinegar such as white wine, rice, or champagne
⅓ cup Simple Syrup (page 47)

Combine all ingredients in a sterilized airtight jar and refrigerate, gently shaking before use to incorporate.

To use in a drink, start with 1 ounce of drinking vinegar for every 6 ounces of drink, less if what you are using is already sour. Adjust to taste.

VARIATIONS:

- Use Flavored Simple Syrup (page 49) or vinegar.

- Add a fruit purée or macerate fruit in vinegar first.

∼ All-Weather Grenadine ∼

True grenadine, made from pomegranates, is hard to find. Most of the commercial versions labeled "grenadine" list ingredients of just corn syrup boosted with more sugars and flavors. The real stuff tastes extra intense, not for the Shirley Temple at heart. Because of the kiddie cocktail and the cheapo versions available, grenadine has come to mean . . . less, but you can change that. This recipe accommodates any sour or tart red fruit. The raspberry leaf layers on a fresher, more complex flavor. Remember: You can always correct with simple syrup, so err on the side of tartness.

Makes 1 cup

2 cups pomegranate juice
2 tablespoons raspberry leaf
1 cup sugar
1 tablespoon 80-proof or higher alcohol (optional)

Bring the pomegranate juice and raspberry leaf to a boil and simmer over medium-low heat until reduced by half.

Strain and add the sugar, stirring until dissolved.

Remove the mixture from the heat and let it cool. Strain into a sterilized, airtight bottle or jar, and if desired, add alcohol as a preservative.

Refrigerate and use within 1 month, 2 months if adding alcohol. It also stores well in the freezer and doesn't freeze into a solid.

WINTER CRANBERRIES

For a winterized, more puckering version of grenadine, use the following recipe.

Makes 1 cup

2 cups water
1½ cups fresh cranberries
1 whole cinnamon stick
2 tablespoons dried hibiscus petals

1 cup sugar
1 tablespoon 80-proof or higher alcohol (optional)

Bring the water, cranberries, cinnamon stick, and hibiscus petals to a boil and simmer over medium-low heat until the mixture is reduced by half.

Strain and add the sugar, stirring until dissolved.

Remove the mixture from the heat and let it cool. Strain into a sterilized, airtight bottle or jar, and if desired, add the alcohol as a preservative.

Refrigerate and use within 1 month, 2 months if adding alcohol. It also stores well in the freezer and doesn't freeze into a solid.

SUMMER CHERRIES

Here's something to splash into just about any citrus-laden drink.

Makes 1 cup

2 cups water
1½ cups fresh pitted cherries (try to get sour cherries)
2 tablespoons fresh pummeled sage leaf
½ cup sugar (or more, depending on sweetness of cherries)
1 tablespoon 80-proof or higher alcohol (optional)

Bring the water, cherries, and sage to a boil and simmer over medium-low heat until the mixture is reduced by half.

Strain and add the sugar, stirring until dissolved.

Remove from the heat and let the mixture cool. Strain into a sterilized, airtight bottle or jar, and if desired, add the alcohol as a preservative.

Refrigerate and use within 1 month, 2 months if adding alcohol. It also stores well in the freezer and doesn't freeze into a solid.

◅ Gentian Tincture ▻

If you ever make one tincture, this is the mother: the opposite of sunshine in a bottle. This tincture is an expression of pure kitten claws on your tongue—bitterness that will produce an involuntary reaction, indubitably. I'll let curiosity eat away on what type of reaction. The usefulness of this tincture is twofold: you'll never have to forget to take the gentian out of an infusion, thus ruining it for the palate of any live mammal; and you'll be able to control the bitterness of anything you produce. This could be the building block of any bitters recipe without adding any more bitter herbs or substances.

Makes 1 cup

1 cup vodka
2 tablespoons cup gentian root

Combine the vodka and gentian root in a jar and let macerate for up to 4 weeks.

Strain the gentian from the vodka and store the resultant tincture in a sterilized, airtight jar at room temperature, labeled clearly to avoid any future vodka tonic mishaps.

You can make a tincture for any herb or spice, to use singly or to add to other recipes. Check your tincture every few days for aroma and flavor since every herb and spice will have a different rate of infusion.

∾ Garnishes ∾

I'm not spending much time on garnishes because I think a drink is like a plate. Don't put anything on or in your drink that doesn't add to it, and don't include something people won't eat. The unfussy power of a proper peel can't be denied, but what the hell am I supposed to do with a rosemary sprig? Bless something?

With garnish, I go citrus or I go seasonal. Any drink I list without a garnish takes the peel of a lemon or most appropriate citrus. This simple rule has many variations, from candied peels and pickled peaches to extra pepper mills filled with favorite spices. I may keep a jar of boozy cherries and a special, doctored jar of olives for *my* martinis (recipes to follow), but that's as crafty as I get. I think it's the drink people should remember, not the peeled grape studded in cloves and sprinkled with gold dust. No, sadly, I didn't make that up.

Seasonal Garnish Ideas

Fall: apple, pear, fig, grapes
Winter: citrus, pomegranate, cranberry
Spring: rhubarb, strawberry
Summer: berries, melon, apricot, peach, cherry

Following are nine uncomplicated recipes for things to put in your drinks.

⤳ Candied Citrus Peel ⤶

A pox on all fruitcakes for demonizing the joy that is candied fruit. Not only can you spear and stick slices of glassy sweet peel into a sour, you can garnish cakes, ice cream, cookies, roasted anything, fish, salad, cheese plates, and so much more. How much you make depends on how much you want, and how you cut the peels. Pick the best-looking citrus you can find. In making Limoncello (page 117) and infusions, the white pith should be avoided for the most part, but here you want to grab a little bit of it to add bitterness, or all of it if you're so inclined. This recipe is my favorite combination.

Makes 2 cups

3 cups Simple Syrup (page 47)
1 cup water
Peel from 4 whole grapefruit, cut to desired shape and size
1 teaspoon coriander
1 teaspoon pink peppercorns
4 whole fresh bay leaves (don't use dried)

Bring the simple syrup and water to a boil in a heavy saucepan. Add the grapefruit peel, coriander, peppercorns, and bay leaves. Simmer on low for 30 minutes.

Remove from the heat and let cool. Transfer to a sterilized, airtight jar.

You can keep the peels in the syrup and remove and cut as needed; they'll stay soft and looking like stained glass. You can separate the peel and simple syrup and use the latter to flavor drinks.

The separated peel will last for many weeks on its own, drying out slowly. You can slice and then shake the dried peel with granulated sugar for a traditional candy shop presentation.

- Use honey syrup or brown sugar syrup for a richer flavor.

- Get creative and use any of your favorite spice combinations and citrus, depending on what drinks you want to garnish:

    —Orange with cinnamon and clove for a manhattan

    —Lemon with sage in honey syrup for rusty nails and Rob Roys

    —Lime with juniper and cinnamon for gimlets

ᘒ Pickled Things #1, Sweet ᘒ

Entire books exist about pickling, but this is not one of them. Quick pickle means you will use that which is pickled within a short period of time. Not suitable for the bomb shelter. For our purposes, we talk about a quick garnish that's smack in-your-face delicious in a simple vodka lemonade or gin and tonic or as complicated an après-work porch cocktail as you want to make. Also righteous on a cheese plate. Monkey with it at will. For the sake of ambiguous pronouns, we'll say the recipe below is for pickled plums.

Makes about 2 cups

2 cups pitted and sliced plums
¼ cup kosher salt
1 cup water
1 cup light vinegar such as white wine, rice, or champagne
⅓ cup sugar
1 tablespoon coriander seed
2 teaspoons mustard seed
1 teaspoon juniper berries
5 allspice berries
2 star anise
1 cinnamon stick

Wash, prep, and slice the fruit you wish to pickle—the softer the produce the thicker the slices so they don't break up. Place them in a colander or your large mesh strainer.

Coat the slices with the salt and put the colander over a bowl or in the sink while the salt draws out moisture. After 1 to 2 hours, rinse the slices and pat dry with paper towels.

While the slices are draining, in a saucepan combine the water, vinegar, sugar, coriander seed, mustard seed, juniper berries, allspice berries, star anise, and cinnamon stick; bring to a boil. Let boil for 5 minutes.

Reduce the heat to a simmer for 20 minutes; remove from the heat.

Put the slices in a sterilized glass jar and pour in the liquid to cover, leaving ½ inch of room if possible. Cover with an airtight lid and refrigerate immediately. Use within 6 weeks.

∿ Pickled Things #2, Savory ∿

Otherwise known as "things you want to put in a Bloody Mary," this recipe is for the savory side of cocktails and can be used to make things for martinis, highballs, and whatever else strikes you as needing a pucker or two. For the sake of pronouns, we'll use daikon sticks as an example. I love the stuff, but be careful: daikon is stinky. (It's also good as a sweet pickle.)

Makes about 2 cups

2 cups daikon, sliced into ¼-inch matchsticks (length determined by how you plan to use them)
¼ cup kosher salt
1 cup water
1 cup light vinegar such as white wine, rice, or champagne
2 teaspoons sugar
1 tablespoon coriander seed
1 tablespoon mustard seed
1 tablespoon dill seed
1 teaspoon fennel seed

Wash, prep, and slice the veggies you wish to pickle into matchsticks (or any small chunky shape)—the softer the produce the thicker the slices so they don't break up. Place them in a colander or your large mesh strainer.

Coat the matchsticks with the salt and put the colander over a bowl or in the sink while the salt draws out moisture. After 1 to 2 hours, rinse the slices and pat dry with paper towels.

While the sticks are draining, in a saucepan combine the water, vinegar, sugar, coriander seed, mustard seed, dill seed, and fennel seed and bring to a boil. Let boil for 5 minutes.

Reduce to a simmer for 20 minutes; remove from the heat.

Put the matchsticks in a sterilized glass jar and pour in the liquid to cover, leaving ½ inch of room if possible. Cover with an airtight lid and refrigerate immediately. Use within 6 weeks.

⌒ Boozy Cherries ⌒

We all by now avoid the unnatural Frankenblobs found in most bars. Maybe that's no great shakes for you, but cherries are my favorite things in the world, so I require a suitable replacement in my manhattan. Proper maraschino cherries are a truly wonderful thing—sour cherries preserved in maraschino, a liquor made in Croatia or Italy from the *maraska* cherry. It takes a committed person to achieve them these days because of the rarity of sour cherries. Even in Washington State we must eagle-eye the farmers' markets.

You can buy a sweetened, imported version from Italy for approximately one arm and half a leg and French *griottes*, tiny cherries in sweet brandy solution, for slightly less, but they are both difficult to find, and boozy cherries are fairly easy to approximate. You can also tailor them to the cocktail they'll garnish. Here are two fixes of varying degrees of effort to help keep your cocktails garnished and you off the little red freaks.

FRESH BOOZY CHERRIES

Makes 2 cups

¼ cup Simple Syrup (page 47)
2 cups fresh, pitted cherries, sour or sweet
Juice and rind of ¼ small lemon
½ teaspoon vanilla tincture or ½ spent vanilla bean pod (optional, see Note)
1½ cups high quality brandy, bourbon, or whiskey, divided

In a small saucepan, bring the simple syrup, cherries, lemon juice and rind, and vanilla to a simmer. Add ½ cup of the liquor and simmer for 20 minutes.

Remove from the heat. Add the remaining 1 cup of liquor and let the mixture cool completely.

Transfer to a sterilized, airtight jar and refrigerate.

Note: Vanilla gives the cherries a bit of flavor, but nothing near the almond-extract–loaded taste of the neon blobs of our youth.

DRIED BOOZY CHERRIES

Makes 1 cup

¾ cup dried cherries (preferably unsweetened; sour is even better)
1 cup high-quality brandy, bourbon, or whiskey
2 tablespoons Simple Syrup (page 47) (see Note)
½ spent vanilla bean pod (optional)

Combine the cherries, liquor, simple syrup, and vanilla bean pod in a 16-ounce sterilized, airtight jar. Wait until the cherries plump up with the booze and then use them. Keep refrigerated.

Note: You can always add a little bit more simple syrup, but try the cherries first.

⤳ Improved Cocktail Olives ⤳

If you want the best olive for a martini and care not about the money, "invest in an olive pitter and Castelvetranos." (This is the seven-word recipe in the book.) Sicily's greatest gift to gin and the culinary world. This is what we do at our bar, but I am far too lazy and cheap on my own time.

Too often jarred olives may add more salt than flavor to a drink, but you can quickly boost their usefulness by adding flavors you like in your gin. These ingredients are all optional and have different uses: Coriander and caraway seeds boost the herbal character. The lemon gives the resulting martini a built-in twist, the peppercorns zing, and a jalapeño will add manageable spice, which is far less than if the olives came stuffed with peppers.

Makes 1 jar

1 jar pitted olives with pimento
1 to 2 cups of your favorite dry vermouth
1 tablespoon coriander, caraway seeds, or peppercorns
Zest or peel of 1 lemon
1 jalapeño, chopped

Drain half the brine from the jar of olives. Replace the other half with the vermouth. Add the remaining ingredients to your liking. That's it.

⤙ Pickled Watermelon Rind ⤛

Of all the items to include, this makes my Top Ten. This rind is good for any tangy drink, better with a drink made from the watermelon's own juices (see Picnic Gin, page 157). You can also add this to a modified Greek salad or lettuces to give people a little shock. The average 4- or 5-pound watermelon will yield more than 1½ pounds of rind; this recipe will use about a quarter of the oblong fruit.

Makes 2 cups

    2 cups watermelon rind
    2 tablespoons salt
    1 cup water
    ½ cup light vinegar such as white wine, rice, or champagne
    ⅓ cup sugar
    1 teaspoon coriander seed
    1 teaspoon fennel seed
    1 teaspoon caraway seeds
    3 quarter-size slices fresh gingerroot

Wash, prep, and slice the rind—¼ inch thick, about 4 inches long.

Coat the rind with the salt and put it in a colander over a bowl or in the sink while the salt draws out moisture. After 1 to 2 hours, rinse the slices and pat dry with paper towels.

While the rinds are draining, combine the water, vinegar, sugar, coriander seed, fennel seed, caraway seeds, and gingerroot in a saucepan and bring to a boil. Let boil for 5 minutes.

Reduce to a simmer for 20 minutes; remove from the heat.

Put the rind in a sterilized glass jar and pour in the liquid to cover, leaving ½ inch of room if possible. Cover with an airtight lid and refrigerate immediately. Let flavors marry for a few days. Use within 6 weeks.

⌁ Cocktail Onions ⌁

This one matters to drinkers of Gibsons only, and maybe an occasional Bloody Mary lover. Cocktail onions are an all-too-common afterthought in most bars, a tiny jar half-full of pale and peeling spheres fading in the back of the beer cooler. Yes, this recipe asks you to buy and peel your own fresh pearl onions or even small cippolinis, but these are difficult to find for many. Frozen pearl onions fit in the same category as frozen peas; it's always OK. If you're into canning, you can process the jar in a water bath for storing at room temperature or for gift giving.

Makes 2 cups

2 cups pearl onions, ½ to 1 inch in diameter
⅓ cup salt, sea or kosher
2 cups light vinegar such as white wine, rice, or champagne
2 tablespoons sugar
Peel of 1 medium lemon
1 teaspoon coriander
¼ cup water
½ sliced jalapeño or small dried chile (optional)

If you are using fresh onions, peel and trim them to the desired size, removing at least the first outer layer. Again, if using fresh onions, brine the onions overnight: Place them in a glass bowl with the salt and enough water to cover. Use a small plate to keep the onions submerged. (Brining softens the onions and takes a bit of the sting out.) Skip the brining step if using frozen pearl onions.

Combine the vinegar, sugar, lemon peel, coriander, and jalapeño in a saucepan with the water and bring to a boil. Let boil for 5 to 10 minutes; reduce to a simmer for 20 minutes.

Meanwhile, drain and pat the onions dry. Transfer them into the smallest jar possible. They should fit snuggly, but leave plenty of room for the vinegar solution.

Pour the vinegar solution into the jar, leaving ½ inch of head space. Allow to cool; seal and refrigerate. Give the mix 1 or 2 weeks for the flavors to marry.

⌁ Freshly Cracked Spices ⌁

Purists would say a smatter of ground anything can foul up a drink's mouthfeel, but a crack or two of fresh cardamom or grains of paradise on top of a Pisco Sour (see page 140) gives the middle finger to that argument. Though I would agree—it's a weird flourish for a clear or completely spirituous drink.

You can buy extra peppermills anywhere—from the home store to the thrift store. If you like Bloody Marys, keep one with coarse salt and dill or celery seed to add a bright initial kick to them. For drinks with fruit juice, you can add a savory touch, like adding some cracked fennel to a Greyhound, or a Perro Salado (page 162).

⚲ **Frozen Stuff** ⚲

My favorite cocktail is a negroni. Served up, I like only the middle—the first sips are too cold and the last too warm. But when I drink a negroni on the rocks, especially in the summer, it waters down too fast. So I decided to go with it and put flavor in the water, freezing grapefruit juice into ice cubes. My negroni still morphs into something else when it melts, but with better results. You can freeze any sort of fruit juice or -ade into cubes and give new meaning to the long drink.

What with what, regarding freezing the following:

Grapes: bob up and down in a glass of bubbly
Lemonade: great with bourbon and soda or any highball
Orange juice: pour vodka and a splash of akvavit for a slightly more
banging Harvey Wallbanger
Limeade: make one with little sugar and plop into a tequila neat
Vermouth: the laziest martini ever

PART TWO:

THE SEASONS

Sparkling Jack Rose cocktail (page 97),
made with Apple Brandy Liqueur (page 96)

Equipment & Prep (page 29)

Infusions: Liquors, Liqueurs & Tinctures (page 41)

For cocktail recipes, see Part Two:
The Seasons (page 81)

Corn & Oil cocktail (page 169),
made with Falernum (page 168)

～ Fall ～

BREWED GINGER BEER
Moscow Mule

MULLED WINE

MEAD (HONEY WINE)

WASSAIL

HONEYED SCOTCH
Love Potion #π

APPLE BRANDY LIQUEUR
Sparkling Jack Rose

AMARO MADE "SIMPLE"

FENNEL LIQUEUR
Pimm's Garden

PLUM SEMICORDIAL
Plum Daisy

ROOT BEER BITTERS
Blackstrapped Manhattan

↜ Brewed Ginger Beer ↝

Remember when I promised that if you could whip up your own salad dressing you could accomplish any recipe in the book? I lied. The phrase "there lie dragons" comes to mind when veering into this territory. It's dangerously close to the land of home brew in the kingdom of nerd that is beer, but it's well worth the effort. Like the first time you tackled baking your own bread, it may not turn out. OK, it may explode. But like the first time you made your own bread, you will feel an immense sense of accomplishment. And you may get hooked. This beer is nothing like what you buy in the store. Expect a far lighter fizz, with less sugar than ginger ale and an attack of spice.

Special equipment: Sterilized glass containers in which to store ginger beer for the final step. This recipe makes one gallon, convenient when using two half-gallon growlers worth, the preferred vessel of choice since they easily fit in a fridge. A strong seal is important, and you want to make sure each container gets a fair portion of yeast. Make sure all containers are glass, sturdy, and sterilized.

Makes 1 gallon

Zest and juice of 6 limes, divided
12 cups filtered water, divided
1 cup finely grated fresh gingerroot
1 cup sugar, preferably turbinado or light brown
½ ounce champagne yeast, divided

Zest the limes into large strips and set aside.

In a large, heavy saucepan, combine 6 cups of the water with the ginger and zest. Bring to a boil; add the sugar, stirring until dissolved.

Let the mixture steep for 10 minutes; reduce to a simmer. Simmer for 15 minutes; remove from the heat.

Allow the mixture to cool before removing the zest. Strain the remaining mixture through a colander into a container large enough to hold it with room to spare (at least 1½ gallons). You want a little flotsam of ginger. Unless you don't. In that case use a fine mesh strainer.

Add the lime juice and the remaining 6 cups of water. Divide the mixture into the 2 sterilized growlers and add half the yeast to each. Agitate gently to marry the yeast with the rest of the ingredients.

Store at room temperature for up to 36 hours, checking on carbonation a few times during this period. (It's essential to let some gas escape.)

You can now refrigerate your growlers of ginger beer for 1 week to 10 days, but you will need to open the bottles at least every other day to burp them. If you don't trust yourself with such vigilance, you can quickly strain the ginger beer off its sediment and into smaller glass jars, bottles, etc.

MOSCOW MULE

A highball of vodka and ginger beer over ice, the Moscow Mule is a boring drink. But if you went to the trouble of making your own ginger beer, don't cover a damn thing up.

> 1½ ounces vodka
> 4 or more ounces Brewed Ginger Beer

Just add ice and your zip code.

WHAT MAKES A GINGERY BREW

Tilson of Books & Bridges Ginger Ale

Nobody knows Tilson's last name. He's our emcee friend who is most likely a visiting alien judging the future of our species. Also, he makes ginger beer. We didn't believe him at first, so I ordered six cases for the restaurant to call the bluff. Then he began talking about scaling production and labels and I was hooked. Thank god the stuff is fantastic.

I have very strong opinions about ginger ales and brews. Good ginger ale starts with a ton of the stuff, as fresh as possible. Tilson and I agree, and we also believe something else, and it's what makes his ginger brew unique and addictive—it's the lime. Allow him to explain.

Ginger the root to all tasty!

> "The cool thing about the lime in ginger ale is it will change where you taste the ginger in the drink (start, middle, or end). You can add a bit of extra lime or lemon and enjoy the flava more. The fun thing about ginger is like a true love or anger it can make you feel warm inside. Let the heat hug your buds of taste, eyes open or closed this kiss was meant to be. Everyone wants to pair ginger and lemon together, but they don't even know."

That's right, Celestial Seasonings. Your Lemon Zinger is a lie. Lime Zinger, more like. (Coincidentally, lime oil is one of the notes that gives Coca-Cola its identifiable flavor.)

⮝ Mulled Wine ⮟

I have two Crock-Pots. When I have people over during the long, soggy winter, I make sure one is filled with pork and the other, wine. I think it's the magic cure for Seasonal Affective Disorder. I look in the boxed wine section for pinot noir, or I ask the wine buyer for something I can see through. It's important to use a lighter, fruitier red wine. Even with cheap stuff, it's still about the right kind of cheap stuff. Maybe you normally drink cabernet and other red wines with tannin, but warm tannic wine makes exactly no one happy.

Makes sixteen 6-ounce punch cups

3 liters (1 box) light red wine
2 cups Simple Syrup, plain or spiced (pages 47 and 50)
2 whole oranges, sliced into discs
6 whole cinnamon sticks
1 tablespoon ground cloves
3 tablespoons freshly minced gingerroot

In a large pot, combine the wine, simple syrup, oranges, and cinnamon sticks. Place the cloves and ginger in a disposable tea bag or a tea ball and add to the pot.

Heat the mixture over medium-low heat for 20 minutes, then lower the heat to a low simmer. (Low heat is important with red wine.) After 1 hour remove the spices. Keep the mixture warm in a heatproof carafe or a Crock-Pot set on low.

TO SERVE

Ladle into coffee cups or small, sturdy glasses. Leftover mulled wine keeps in the refrigerator for up to 4 days.

VARIATIONS:

- Use your own favorite spice mix and replace all or any of the above spices with cardamom, coriander, star anise, nutmeg, etc.

- Substitute 1 cup apple juice for 1 cup simple syrup for less sweet results; add 1 cup apple juice to simple syrup for more flavor.

- To make the Swedish version of mulled wine—Glögg—simmer with raisins and skinned almonds.

- Start each cup with a splash of brandy or bourbon.

- For a personalized date version (or party of one), use 1 bottle wine, ½ cup simple syrup, and half the spices.

∽ Mead (Honey Wine) ∾

I would be cheating you if I didn't include a recipe for the unofficial beverage of my people (*cough*, nerds). Also, I wrote this season drinking my own meadly wares; it's only apropos. Mead has a history damn near as old as civilization and is so simple even a serf can do it. Also, it's effing fantastic. This recipe is my remedial Mead 101 variation based on the recipe included in the renowned Charlie Papazian's *The Complete Joy of Home Brewing*. I simplified it after realizing the title of this book to be . . . ironic.

Makes 1 gallon

1 gallon water
1 quart honey
Zest and juice of 2 oranges
1 cup Earl Grey tea, extra strong
3 whole allspice berries
Champagne yeast

Bring the water to a boil in a large stockpot. Remove from the heat, add the honey, and stir well.

Add the zest, juice, tea, and allspice berries. Let the mixture steep until cool. Pour into a sterilized 1-gallon jar and add the yeast.

Let the mixture ferment for 2 weeks, burping daily. Slowly strain into whatever size sterilized bottles with airtight lids you wish to store or gift. Recycled ceramic-stoppered beer bottles are perfect, as are growlers (page 184). Store the bottles in a refrigerator or a cool basement.

VARIATIONS:

- Lager yeast works as well as champagne yeast for flavor and higher alcohol.

- Feel free to substitute your favorite spice or none at all.

- Using honey from a specific plant, like lavender or raspberry, will add subtle flavor.

- Substitute your favorite tea (try blackberry), or omit altogether.

ᴥ Wassail ᴥ

Wassail may belong to holidays and winter in the modern day, but its roots run pagan, and fall is cider time: "Here we go a wassailing . . ." It's not just a drink; it's a verb, a greeting to be exact. Wassailing is the old English tradition of celebrating the harvest. Many variations of wassail exist, but tradition-ally it's a cider- or ale-based drink, or both, combined with eggs, apples, and spices. However you make it, a correct wassail is the right answer to the question, "What would a hobbit drink?"

The whole point of a punch, especially this one, is to use what you have on hand, so raid your spice jars. You want baking spices, pumpkin pie spices. My rule: if you've seen it in a coffee cake, it can go in hot cider. Just mind the measure with more pungent spices (e.g., cloves).

Punch strength: ¾-ounce liquor per serving.

Makes sixteen 6-ounce servings

9 cups apple cider
¼ cup minced fresh gingerroot
4 lemons, sliced
3 cinnamon sticks
1 spent vanilla bean
1½ cups bourbon

In a large saucepan, combine the cider, gingerroot, lemons, cinnamon sticks, and vanilla bean. Simmer on low for at least 1 hour, until the flavor tastes good to you.

Use a ratio of 5 ounces punch to ¾ ounce bourbon. Use a marked shot glass to keep consistent when adding the bourbon and for guests to self-pour when you're not around.

Serve from the stove or keep warm in a carafe.

- Adjust the cider to include brown ale or completely substitute cider for ale, according to personal taste.

- Intensify the flavor by using spiced bourbon.

I think a good host makes weak punch or tells people exactly how much is in a serving. It's the right thing to do.

Octane levels: A martini or a manhattan don't count as one drink. As served in most bars, the "M" words contain at least a drink and a half (more if you make your manhattan with 100-proof Rittenhouse). Your glass of wine doesn't go to your head the same all the time either, depending on how big your glass. We often count what we've drunk by the glass. Know before you go this holiday season: one drink = 1½ ounce 80-proof liquor (40% ABV); 6 ounces of wine (approximately 14% ABV); one 12-ounce beer (approximately 5% ABV), where ABV means "alcohol by volume."

∿ Honeyed Scotch ∿

I have a secret mission in life: to get chicks to drink more Scotch and less fruity -tinis, just like our no-nonsense grannies did. One of my favorite drinks of all time is the Rusty Nail: Scotch whiskey with Drambuie on the rocks. It's at once earthy and floral with a touch of honey sweet. Drambuie is Scotch whiskey steeped in secret herbs and spices and sweetened with heather honey. I wish it was a little less sweet. Like this:

Makes 3 cups

6 mace blades
1½ teaspoon anise seed
3 cups Scotch whiskey
1 teaspoon lavender
¼ to ⅓ cup light agave nectar (see Note)

Crush the mace and anise seed in a mortar and pestle. Combine with the whiskey and lavender in a sterilized jar and let macerate for 2 weeks, shaking daily.

Double strain the mixture and sweeten with the agave nectar to taste. (Err on the side of less sweet; the liqueur will develop a bit in the bottle.) Bottle in a sterilized, airtight jar or bottle and store in the fridge for longer life.

Note: Use agave instead of honey because you won't need to make a simple syrup, which will keep the alcohol at its full strength.

Variations:

- Substitute ½ cup honey syrup using a flower-specific local honey.

LOVE POTION #π

Apparently one of the most enticing aromas for the average male is pumpkin pie, even more so when mixed with lavender, according to a study by Dr. Alan R. Hirsch of the Smell and Taste Treatment and Research Foundation in Chicago. I also heard it mentioned on *Oprah* once, so it must be true. This recipe started as a joke, a joke that went horribly, awfully . . . right, but this author makes no claim or guarantee of bewitchment.

    4 to 8 ounces hot Earl Grey tea
    1½ ounces Honeyed Scotch
    1 cinnamon stick (optional)

Combine the tea and Scotch in a large snifter or Irish coffee glass. Garnish with a cinnamon stick if you like. Use more or less tea, depending on if it's pre- or après ski.

⤳ Apple Brandy Liqueur ⤳

The first commercial distillery in America, Laird & Company, was and still is dedicated to apple brandy and applejack. So the saying should really go, "As American as apple brandy." Use your favorite apples in this recipe, the tarter the better. I use Granny Smiths. You can add a splash of the liqueur to your favorite whiskey or whiskey cocktail, or substitute for any like-minded liquor in desserts.

Makes 3 cups

2 cups brandy or bourbon
4 medium apples
1 cup Simple Syrup (spiced, if desired) (page 47)

Put the brandy into a large wide-mouth, sterilized jar. (You don't have to cut the apples in round sections, but it sure does look ten times cooler.)

Slice the apples into approximately ¼-inch slices, reserving the cores. Fit as many slices as you can submerge into the brandy and secure with a small plate or nonporous object to keep the slices submerged.

Heat the simple syrup, adding the leftover cores and apple bits. Let the mixture simmer on low for up to 1 hour, turn off the heat, and add the mixture to the brandy and apples.

Let sit for 2 weeks in a cool, dark place, gently shaking daily, then double strain (preferably with a coffee filter) and transfer to a large, sterilized, airtight jar or wine bottle.

VARIATIONS:

- If using apple brandy, omit the simple syrup.

- Making spiced apple brandy means you will have the easiest drink in the world on hand for surprise guests—just add hot water and lemon. Use a combination of your favorite spices, but I keep it simple with a few whole cinnamon sticks and pieces of star anise.

SPARKLING JACK ROSE

The Jack Rose is a fine enough cocktail, but when dealing with home-made apple brandy, the bubbles here help magnify the fresher tree fruit aroma and flavor, turning fine to memorable. I use sour cherry grenadine made from Washington State cherries to really make it a local affair, but it's all about the apples.

  1½ ounce Apple Brandy Liqueur
  ¼ ounce lime juice
  ½ ounce cherry grenadine (see page 65)
  3 to 4 ounces bubbly
  1 apple slice

Combine apple brandy, lime juice, and grenadine in a shaker with ice. Shake and strain into a champagne glass, and top with the bubbly. Garnish with a thin slice of apple.

VARIATIONS:

- Substitute apple purée for the grenadine for a boozier apple version of a Bellini.

- Substitute dry sparkling cider—French from Normandy or English. Dry only; anything else is too sweet.

∿ Amaro Made "Simple" ∾

Amaro means bitter in Italian, which has always made me smile because of its proximity to the word for love, *amore*. The flavor bitter is the least palatable to the average American palate, the ultimate acquired taste. In cocktails it shines, countering sour and sweet and pulling everything together like a perfect bass line. Some amaro can be a bit harsh, like the minty and licorice medicinal notes of Fernet Branca and Jagermeister, but there is an entire category of amber amaros, like Averna and Rammazoti, that taste like boozy, unsweetened versions of cola or root beer. Keep in mind: these liqueurs are very complex and are made by distilling with oil and spices, adding highly concentrated essential oils. The home version will always taste like faint copies. Start with this recipe and adjust the sweet and savory spices to fit your taste.

Makes 3 cups

1 teaspoon cardamom
2 whole star anise
6 fresh bay leaves
6 fresh sage leaves
2½ cups brandy or whiskey
Zest of 2 oranges, thick, with a bit of white pith
1 tablespoon minced gingerroot
½ cinnamon stick (2-inch length)
¼ teaspoon gentian root
1 teaspoon sarsaparilla
1 cup water
½ cup dark brown sugar

Lightly crush the cardamom and star anise with the bay and sage leaves to release the oils. Combine with the brandy, zest, ginger, and cinnamon stick in a jar and macerate for 1 week, shaking daily.

Add the gentian and sarsaparilla and let macerate 1 week, again shaking daily.

Strain the solids from the infusion. Bring the water and all the strained herbs and spices to a boil; add the brown sugar and stir until dissolved. Turn the heat to low and simmer until the liquid reduces by half. Let cool.

Double strain the sweetened mixture and combine with the alcohol infusion. Keep in a sterilized, airtight jar or bottle at room temperature and allow the mixture to marry for at least another week before drinking. Store in the refrigerator.

TO SERVE

Serve slightly chilled before or after a meal. For brunch, serve in equal parts with grapefruit juice on the rocks. As an aperitif, pour over rocks and add a splash of soda or ginger ale with a big slice of orange. After a meal, sip straight.

VARIATIONS:

- For extra flavor, add 1 tablespoon blackstrap or regular molasses to the simple syrup.

YOU SAY AMARO, I SAY JAGER

Many the bartender who nods approvingly when you order a shot of chilled Fernet Branca will silently berate you if you ordered one of Jagermeister. Yet the two are the same, both herbal liqueurs that act as tonics to help aid in digestion and make wicked work on any stomachache. It's true, one shot of either after an evening of gluttony and you're ready for another feast thirty minutes later. The only difference: the secret blend of herbs and spices that make one liqueur more minty and the other more akin to black licorice, as well as their respective marketing departments. Look at Fernet Branca as the sister who'd be beadless at Mardi Gras, and look at the bartender and ask him what he has against Germans.

✕ Fennel Liqueur ✕

Seattle in the fall—you can't throw a rock without hitting something to forage or a fleece vest. (If you forage, remember to pick above the dog's leg and away from the street.) I use it as an opportunity to get my hands on all the wild fennel I can for pickling... it and me.

Finocchietto: If I got the ending of the word right, it's a common homemade liqueur in Italy. If I got it wrong, it's a little boy whose nose sprouts fennel when he lies. I always looked at this liqueur as the Sicilian answer to akvavit, and it is known to aid in digestion.

Fennel is also one of the most common ingredients in gripe water, which is a similar infusion to the recipe that follows and is used to help babies with their colic and fussing. It could also be used to soothe similarly fussy customers in the restaurant, one supposes...

Makes 3 cups

Three 8-inch-long stalks wild fennel or 1 whole fennel bulb
2 cups high-proof vodka (100-proof or higher)
1 cup Simple Syrup (page 47), or more

Break down the fennel into bite-size chunks. Combine the fennel and vodka in a large, wide- mouth jar. Let the infusion macerate for 5 days in a cool, dark place.

Strain the mixture and add the simple syrup to taste.

Divvy up the mixture into sterilized, airtight bottles and jars and store at room temperature, or keep in the freezer for optimal serving temperature.

Unlike akvavit, which is awesome straight out of the freezer, this liqueur has a more delicate aroma and flavor that you don't want to shoot down with such a chill. Serve with just a few rocks.

PIMM'S GARDEN

Dedicated to the negroni fan, this drink stands in for when a Pimm's cup just isn't strong enough.

    1½ ounces Pimm's
    1 ounce Fennel Liqueur
    Dash Citrus Bitters (page 127)

Combine the Pimm's, liqueur, and bitters with ice; stir and strain into a cocktail glass or a rocks glass filled with fresh ice. Use a larger glass and add soda for a long drink.

HERBAL PERFECTION, NERD INSPIRATION

Marc Bernhard, owner of Pacific Distillery in Woodinville, Washington, is all about the botanicals. Joining the ranks of Boeing nerds supplying our fishing village with alcohol, Bernhard makes a gin, Voyager (that won double Gold in the 2011 San Francisco World Spirits Competition), and an absinthe, Pacifique (which won Gold that same year). Though he works in the flight deck safety department at Boeing, Bernhard used to have a mail-order herb business, so he was keen on what he wanted to use in his spirits and knew where to get them. What he could not get, he grew; not only does he have a backyard lined with wormwood and hyssop, but he's also commandeered plots of land from friends and family to grow herbs. Pacific Distillery is a small, sparsely appointed garage cubicle in a warehouse in the Eastern burbs. The headquarters could barely hold a moving truck but is plenty big enough for a half-dozen stainless steel tanks and Bernhard's striking copper alembic still, which he had custom-built in Portugal. Each herb Bernhard uses is grown, dried, and added in accordance with a few antique distilling manuals he owns. He is determined to uphold traditional practices such as allowing his wormwood to cure for a year before using it in distilling, and these details are evident in the final fiery product.

The first time I tried Bernhard's Pacifique Absinthe, it knocked me out, and not just because I tried it at still strength. The herbal notes of Bernhard's shrewd choices were bloody gorgeous. Pacifique contains two kinds of wormwood, common and Roman, and a hefty portion of a special fennel that allows for more than just anise to shine through. It was that fennel I'd smelled when I first walked into the garage, and it haunted me for weeks. I left that suburban business park and pledged to do better and not settle for just any bulk herb fodder.

Pacific Distillery
18808 142nd Ave NE #4B
Woodinville, WA
www.pacificdistillery.com

Plum Semicordial
∼ (a sweet *slivovitz*) ∼

Some fruit just lends itself better than others to booze. Slivovitz is a traditional Slavic plum brandy, the commercial being a brandy distilled from plums and the homemade being as crude as plums left to ferment in earthen crocks. I don't encourage the use of home pot stills or wild fermentation in the home, so here we'll settle for extra-ripe, dripping-sweet plums soaked in booze.

Makes 3 cups

2 pounds ripe, sweet plums
2½ cups brandy or grappa
½ cup Simple Syrup (page 47), divided

Pit the plums and cut into quarters, at least. Combine with the brandy in a wide-mouth, sterilized jar and let macerate for 3 weeks, shaking every few days.

Double strain the mixture and taste. The sweetness will vary based on the type of plums you've used. Adjust, using a few tablespoons of the simple syrup at a time.

Store in a sterilized, airtight jar or bottle at room temperature. For best results, let the cordial sit for another 2 weeks before serving.

VARIATIONS:

- Squirrels got your plums? You can fudge this recipe with sulfite-free, organic pitted prunes.

PLUM DAISY

A daisy is a lemony take on the margarita, used with your favorite spirit (the most popular being gin). Normally, a daisy would employ ¼ ounce of orange liqueur, but I've omitted it here and subbed in a little bitters, to focus on the plum.

2 ounces Plum Semicordial
¾ ounce lemon juice
¼ ounce Simple Syrup (page 47)
Dash Citrus Bitters (page 127)

Combine all ingredients in a shaker and fill with ice. Shake and strain into a cocktail glass or your favorite glass. Optional: pour over crushed ice.

⌒ **Root Beer Bitters** ⌒

How many of us grew up with that one place—usually a burger joint—that we wanted to go to only for the root beer? My favorite was Dog-n-Suds, which was on the way to Lake Geneva just over the Illinois border in Wisconsin, almost like a cream soda–root beer hybrid. Root beer flavors range from almost butterscotch or rum-butter candy richness—to a very high-toned wintergreen-dominant bite. This recipe tries to strike a chord with as many childhoods as possible.

Makes 2 cups

1½ cups good-quality bourbon
½ vanilla bean, seeded
1 teaspoon grated fresh gingerroot
1 tablespoon sarsaparilla
1 teaspoon dandelion root
1 to 2 star anise
1 cup water
½ tablespoon molasses

Combine the bourbon, vanilla bean, gingerroot, sarsaparilla, dandelion root, and star anise in a large jar. Let the infusion sit for 1 week, shaking it several times daily.

Double strain the bourbon into a large, clean jar and reserve the herbs and spices.

In a small saucepan, bring the water to a boil. Immediately reduce the heat to low, stir in the molasses, and add the reserved herbs and spices. Simmer until the liquid is reduced by half; remove from the heat.

Let the mixture cool; strain through a coffee filter into the bourbon and store in a sterilized, airtight jar at room temperature. The bitters can be used immediately, but shake before using because of the molasses.

BLACKSTRAPPED MANHATTAN

The "black" moniker when added to a manhattan usually refers to the substitution of an Italian amaro liqueur for the sweet vermouth. The swap turns the normally red-tinged amber cocktail into a dark brunette shade. This recipe uses blackstrap molasses and Sicilian Shrubb from the future (i.e., Winter) instead. The result is a whiskey drink fit for the darkest, dimmest corner of the bar or basement.

2 ounces whiskey, preferably rye
¾ ounce Sicilian Shrubb (page 123)
2 dashes Root Beer Bitters
Orange peel, flamed (optional)

Combine the whiskey, shrubb, and bitters in a pint glass. Add ice and stir.

Strain into a cocktail glass and garnish with the orange peel, if so inclined.

TO FLAME AN ORANGE PEEL: Shave a section of orange about one thumb wide and three or four fingers long. Make sure to use a fresh orange, so there's enough oil in the skin. Light a match first. Hold the peel with the orange side over the cocktail glass—carefully between your thumb and index finger (on the shorter side)—and without squeezing in order to save all the oil for the big ooh and aah. Put the lit match between the glass and the peel (a little over a hand's width). Squeeze the peel. Ooh and aah.

SASSAFRAS IS JUST ALL RIGHT WITH HER

Sugarpill Apothecary is a newer addition to Seattle, owned by herbalist and homeopath Karyn Schwartz. The shop's dark wood cabinetry–laden back wall dominates, succinctly stocked with culinary and medicinal herbs as well as tinctures and remedies concocted by Schwartz herself. The shop also carries herbed salts, chocolate, sundries, and a variety of other things to tweak the senses.

I learned long ago that to have a little knowledge of something is almost worse than knowing nothing. When you're macerating an herb in alcohol for weeks on end, you're creating a potentially strong tincture, and it's wise to get a consult. Some herbs might be complementary in aroma, but not make good juju together. (That's me talking hippie.)

Schwartz has worked as an herbalist for years and has a penchant for cocktail bitters. "Sometimes I feel like a bartender to bartenders. They know everything behind their bar and what it can add to a cocktail. It's exactly the same for me," says Schwartz. Only her four ounces goes into an amber bottle and eyedropper.

We talked about my Root Beer Bitters recipe and my want to use sassafras, an FDA-marked carcinogen. "Sassafras is generally contraindicated for anyone pregnant, nursing, or dealing with chronic liver or kidney conditions, cancer, or other serious illnesses," says Schwartz. "If you want a little bit of that sassafras flavor, it's probably fine to add a little in the mix since you will generally be using a minute amount of bitters in a drink, and therefore not something that you will be consuming in large quantities, repeatedly.

"I recommend making separate tinctures of each herb, spice or whatever other ingredients you are thinking about using, and play around with them to see how they complement or detract from one another. Some ingredients offer more than one note once tinctured, and this will help you in the blending process, just like getting to know foods or spices helps you construct more elaborate recipes."

When I showed her my recipe for Root Beer Bitters, I was a little proud to get her approval. She added "If I was going to play with the flavor at all, I'd consider adding a bit of allspice."

Karyn Schwartz
Sugarpill Apothecary
900 East Pine St
Seattle's Capitol Hill neighborhood
www.sugarpillseattle.com

~ Winter ~

SWEET & SAVORY AKVAVIT
Swedish 60

THE PASHA'S RYE

COFFEE LIQUEUR
Bravest Bull

CELLOS
Between the Sheets

ADVOCAAT

BAY LEAF LIQUEUR
The Lemon Drop

SICILIAN SHRUBB
Champagne Punch

NOCINO
Brandy Stout

CITRUS BITTERS
Green Gin

HOMEMADE TONIC
Gin & Homemade Tonic

VODKA SOUP

⌁ Sweet & Savory Akvavit ⌁

Akvavit, like gin, is a catchall term describing a certain range of infused liquors. Just as you expect gin to have at least a hint of juniper, the majority of akvavit has its own accepted herbal and spice characteristics. Caraway leads in most, but many spices can attain the typical candied-fennel-dominant note in akvavit—coriander, anise seed, dill, and juniper included.

Akvavit is more about the place and how it's used. It's a staple of Scandinavian celebrations, especially Christmas, and drinkers pour chilled akvavit into tiny shot glasses, sipping it quickly as they feast on all manner of pickled and smoked fishes. So it's not a stretch to say that any infusion with a combination of the above spices, which are meant to complement the above foods, could be coined *akvavit*.

Here's a stab or two. The first is a more traditional akvavit that's not nearly as sweet as some on the market. I developed it for my dear friend Paula's (a.k.a. international burlesque maven The Swedish Housewife, look her up) annual Christmas Eve party. The second is a savory akvavit that relies more on toasted caraway and layered dill flavors. It will blow your mind with smoked seafood.

Makes more than 3 cups

THE SWEET
3 cups (1 bottle) high-proof vodka (100-proof or higher)
2 tablespoons caraway seeds
2 tablespoons fennel seed
6 to 10 fresh sage leaves
3 allspice berries
¼ to ⅓ cup light agave nectar

Combine the vodka, caraway seeds, fennel seeds, sage leaves, and allspice berries in a large sterilized jar. Let the mixture macerate for 1 week to 10 days, shaking daily.

Strain the mixture and add the agave 1 tablespoon at a time to adjust the sweetness. Store in a sterilized airtight jar or bottle in the freezer. Serve in small shot glasses.

THE SAVORY

¼ cup caraway seeds
3 cups (1 bottle) high-proof vodka (100-proof or higher)
4 fresh dill stalks
2 tablespoons dill seed
1 teaspoon cumin seed
⅛ to ¼ cup light agave nectar

Toast the caraway seeds and combine with the vodka, dill stalks, dill seed, and cumin seed in a large, sterilized jar. Let the mixture macerate for 1 week to 10 days, shaking daily.

Remove the dill stalks and allow the mixture to stand 2 weeks, shaking every few days.

Strain the mixture and add the agave 1 tablespoon at a time to adjust the sweetness. I use 4 teaspoons, max. Store in a sterilized airtight jar or bottle in the freezer. Serve in small shot glasses.

VARIATIONS:

- I love the way agave pairs with these flavors, but simple syrup works too—especially Honey Syrup (page 47). Akvavit is very forgiving, and you can always add sugar or thin it out with more booze.

SWEDISH 60

I'll keep going with what is turning out to be the Northern European bender of a chapter with a take on the classic French 75. Using akvavit—either commercial or your own—makes a slightly richer drink compared to using gin. This recipe uses less sugar because it assumes the akvavit contains some of its own, and lime because it goes better with akvavit. Use Herbal Syrup (page 49) to increase the yule factor.

1½ ounces Akvavit
1 bar spoon Simple Syrup (page 47)
½ ounce lime juice
3 or more ounces sparkling wine
Lime peel

Combine the akvavit, simple syrup, and lime juice in a shaker and fill with ice. Shake and strain into a cocktail or small rocks glass. Top with sparkling wine. Garnish with the lime twist.

ᴖ The Pasha's Rye ᴖ

I have a short list of stand-alone infusions I make. Putting them in cocktails or mixing them with bitters or any other flavor would just hide the already distinct flavors, like putting too much makeup on a pretty girl. Serve this drink neat or, in rare instances, in a snifter heated over a cup of hot water. This drink is named after the Turkish equivalent of an English lord, and it is also a Chicagoland-area bar where things always tend to go . . . sideways. Be careful with whom you share this brew.

Makes 3 cups

3 cups high-proof rye (100-proof or higher)
12 whole dates
10 to 12 small dried rosebuds
1 teaspoon cardamom seeds, lightly crushed
2 mace blades, lightly crushed

Combine the rye, dates, rosebuds, cardamom seeds, and mace in a large jar and agitate every few days for 3 weeks.

Strain into a sterilized, airtight jar or bottle and store at room temperature.

TO SERVE

Infusions don't always need a cocktail recipe. With the Pasha you don't want to cover up even a molecule. You can take a bit of the heat off by pouring it over ice and immediately straining into a small glass or snifter. I put mine in a snifter or wine glass and hold it over some hot water to warm a bit so the aromas will deliver a KO. Like smelling salts for the soul.

⁓ Coffee Liqueur ⁓

I almost completely spaced on putting this recipe in the book. Egg on face that would have been, and this being Seattle, it would have been fresh from someone's backyard chicken coop. This recipe looks remedial, and in preparation that's true. But the quality of the ingredients marks the most crucial step for besting the mass-market coffee liqueurs. It's sublime if you use quality ingredients; don't waste your time if you're scrounging for beans. Use spent vanilla beans to achieve a mellow vanilla flavor; otherwise you'll end up with a harsh, extract-like flavor. Drink it on the rocks or with a little splash of cream and soda water. But don't you dare adulterate it with vodka. I don't care how much you love the Coen brothers.

Special equipment: a French press to achieve the closest thing to freshly pulled espresso.

Makes 4½ cups

3 cups (1 bottle) 80-proof brandy
1 cup best-quality dark roast or espresso coffee, just pressed
1 spent vanilla bean
½ to 1 cup Simple Syrup (page 47), divided

Combine the brandy, coffee, and vanilla bean in a large sterilized jar and let macerate for 3 weeks, shaking every few days.

Strain the brandy mixture and add the simple syrup to taste, ¼ cup at a time. Transfer into sterilized, airtight jars or bottles and store at room temperature.

Serve neat or slightly chilled. Add just a splash of cream to it on the rocks. (This is one of the few times I'd advocate dairy in booze.) You want to highlight the fine coffee flavor, not cover it up.

BRAVEST BULL

A Brave Bull was always our breakfast shot of choice while tailgating. Homemade coffee liqueur—as opposed to store bought—makes this shot far less silly, and almost serious. Seriously good.

1½ ounces tequila
¾ ounce Coffee Liqueur
1 lemon slice, squeezed

Pour the tequila and liqueur over ice with the squeeze of lemon, or shake with ice and serve as a chilled shot.

∼ Cellos ∼

When life gives you lemons, don't shortchange yourself by making lemonade. Make limoncello. More than mere citrus vodka, making a cello—limoncello being the most common—involves extracting all the sensory goodness from lemons. It's like stealing from Mother Nature.

This liqueur uses only the zest of lemons, where the fragrant oils hide; the white pith would foul the aromatic intensity of the liqueur with bitterness, and the juice just clouds up the pure essence of the cello.

Makes about 4 cups

Zest of 8 large lemons
3 cups vodka (approximately 1 bottle), at least 80 proof
1 to 1½ cups Simple Syrup (page 47)

In a large, sterilized mason jar, combine the zest with the vodka and simple syrup. Store in a cool place for up to 4 weeks, shaking daily to help release the oils.

Strain the mixture into a sterilized airtight jar or bottle and store in the freezer for maximum enjoyment. It may also be kept at room temperature.

BETWEEN THE SHEETS

This is one of those drinks probably best forgotten, one that also crosses streams—cane liquor comingling with that of the grape. A homemade cello gives just the right remix.

1 ounce rum
1 ounce Cello
1 ounce cognac or brandy
Splash citrus juice and rind to match the Cello

Combine the rum, cello, cognac, and juice with ice and shake. Strain and garnish with the rind.

～ Advocaat ～

Advocaat liqueur puts the Brandy Alexander in a headlock. It's all creamy protein, no dairy. It's like the breakfast of champions, if that champion were Keith Richards instead of Rocky Balboa. The bonus to this recipe: no waiting for things to steep, marry, or settle. You can even use regular brandy or bourbon, and don't be afraid to pour a little over a slice of cake.

Makes six 2-ounce servings

3 cups water
6 egg yolks
½ cup sugar
2 pinches salt
½ teaspoon good vanilla extract
1¼ cups brandy or whiskey
Grated nutmeg (optional)

Bring the water to a boil in a medium saucepan.

Meanwhile, in a large glass mixing bowl beat the egg yolks with the sugar and salt until the mixture is creamy and smooth, like a very thick sauce. (This is faster in a mixer or blender, but you need to pour the beaten mixture into a glass bowl for the next instruction.) Then, keeping the same speed, slowly add the vanilla and brandy.

Put the glass bowl atop the boiling water, making a double boiler. Hand whisk constantly as the bowl heats. You want the mixture to become thick and warm, not hot. Remove the bowl. Add the nutmeg and refrigerate up to 4 days, heating and rewhisking before serving.

TO SERVE

Serve the advocaat while a little warm in small punch or tea cups, as it's incredibly rich.

- Replace ¼ cup brandy with a suitable spiced or fruity liqueur.
- Use a vanilla-infused brandy or whiskey.

To Have or Not to Have a Happy Holiday Party

Pulling out every bottle from the cabinet ranks as the biggest mistake people make when throwing a holiday party. On the one hand, they end up with friends and family staring at the selection, paralyzed by choice. On the other hand, it's impossible to stock everyone's favorite drink, no matter how many bottles they set on the table. On the third hand, they're borrowing trouble. When laying out the booze for holiday soirées, follow the mantra Keep It Simple (with plenty of ice) Stupid. A few guidelines:

Know your public. If you like wine but your family subsists on bottled beer, be prepared to offer both. Don't worry about catering to every attendee, though; even if your cousin Bob's tastes lean toward gin cocktails, it's perfectly OK to serve beer, whiskey and ginger, or wine and punch only. It's your living room, not a lounge; people will acclimate.

Think long and hard before serving bubbly. Around the holidays, sparkling wine is the one thing no one can resist. It is indeed a perfect treat if you think your crowd can handle it, but bubbles really do go straight to your head. The road to party hell is lined with bottles of bubbly and ruined furniture. If you do it, get small, appropriate cups.

Focus on liquor, never sicker. I am a big fan of punch, but this is also a way to totally F.U.B.A.R. (@$#% Up Beyond All Recognition) your guests. If you do make a punch, do everyone a favor and stray more toward sangria or something with the alcohol content of a wine cooler. People really knock back the punch, and you don't do anyone any favors by playing "Hide the Southern Comfort."

Make sure to post how much alcohol is in each serving of punch. This seems nerdy, but it's more rightly a public service.

Choose for your guests. If you want to serve hard liquor, pick a few bottles and pair them with a few mixers. One type of liquor will suffice, with the trimmings. Example: a couple of big bottles of bourbon and the choice of ginger beer, limeade, and a hot toddy mix in a thermos. Nobody will miss drinking vodka.

Don't try so hard to impress. It's a safe bet that 95 percent of your guests will have no idea what to do with a bottle of St. Germain or have any interest in your bitters collection. I have some really cool stuff in my bar, but I try to remember this lesson. People need that suggestive sell, like that of a cocktail menu, to be enticed into the unknown.

If you want to show off a newfound love of crème de violette or some such swank, pick a drink to offer and post a recipe card your guests can use to mix their own drinks, or premix them in a pitcher. A little Martha goes a long way: your guests won't feel stupid for not knowing what to do, and you get to share fun drinks without having to play bartender all night. The best house cocktail ideas are always a combination of thoughtfulness and laziness. Write out a simple dummy recipe, for example: "Two fingers of applejack. A splash of lime juice. Fill with bitter lemon soda." I also like to note alternatives, such as "also great with spicy ginger ale or lemonade."

Whatever you do, remember that the holidays are about friends and family. Be considerate of your guests, what they like, and offer just enough choice for merriment—but lead them not down the path to the porcelain god.

᚛ Bay Leaf Liqueur ᚜

We have a laurel (bay) tree outside the restaurant where I work, and I sneak the leaves into everything, especially in winter since it's evergreen. It's best steeping in cream for panna cotta or other creamy desserts, which is how I got inspired and started playing with it. Bay is so complementary with sweet that I doggedly set to capturing the taste in a liqueur. A bit savory with the hint of rosemary, I look at bay as the bass to rosemary's treble. Bay lacks the camphor note of the latter and has an addictive, sexy smell like the green equivalent of musk. Sip chilled, substitute for gin in a French 75, or pour a little into a glass of sparkling wine.

Makes 3 cups

   3 to 4 dozen fresh bay leaves (don't use dried)
   Zest of 1 orange
   2¼ cups vodka, at least 80 proof
   ¾ cup Simple Syrup (page 47)

Lightly score or chop the bay leaves. Combine the zest and leaves with the vodka in a large sterilized jar and let steep for 2 to 3 weeks, but no more, agitating every other day. Strain and add the simple syrup to taste. Keep in a sterilized, airtight jar at room temperature.

The flavor here is too subtle to keep in the freezer. To serve chilled, pour the liqueur over ice, stir quickly, and strain.

VARIATIONS:

- In Poland, they make a liqueur called Zubrowka made with sweetgrass. The results are subtle, just as with bay. To make Zubrowka, substitute 1½ cup sweetgrass (just the green leaves) for bay leaves in the above recipe.

THE LEMON DROP

A boozy shot of lemonade, basically. A slam dunk, but somewhere along the line when every drink began to use the suffix "-tini," the lemon drop ended up in a martini glass with a sugared rim, and became the butt of jokes amongst bar snobs. Most bartenders hate making this drink. It's not you, it's us. Get back to your college roots in style.

> 1¼ ounces Bay Leaf Liqueur
> ½ ounce lemon juice

Combine ingredients with ice. Shake like mad and strain into a large shot glass.

∿ Sicilian Shrubb ∿

The bar does not suffer from a lack of orange liqueurs—Cointreau, Grand Marnier, curaçao, etc. One of my favorites is Creole Shrubb, which is unique for being made of *rhum agricole* from Martinique, and this recipe is a nod to it—a cross between a vermouth and an orange liqueur. It takes a manhattan slightly sideways, and adds a different, deeper flavor to a margarita. Use madeira or sherry if you like.

Makes 3 cups

½ cup Simple Syrup (page 47)
1 cup water
Zest and juice of 3 oranges
1 tablespoon bitter orange peel (optional)
1 teaspoon black peppercorns
2 whole star anise
½ cup brandy
2 cups sweet marsala, decent quality

In a saucepan, bring the simple syrup and water to a boil; add the orange zest, orange juice, bitter orange peel, peppercorns, and star anise. Reduce the heat to low and simmer for 20 minutes or until the mixture is reduced by a little more than half.

Remove from the heat, add the brandy, and let cool.

Combine the mixture with the marsala in a large (greater than 24 ounce), sterilized jar. Store in a cool, dry place for 1 week, shaking daily.

Strain the mixture into a sterilized, airtight jar or bottle and refrigerate.

CHAMPAGNE PUNCH

Good punch is hard to find. Release your inner hostess and show your guests they're better than bottles of fruit juice and cheap brandy. Remember, garbage in, garbage out. Chill all the ingredients, which will keep the ice from diluting them too much. A proper hostess would, of course, make an ice mold.

Punch strength: 8 percent alcohol

Makes twenty-eight 6-ounce servings

3 cups Sicilian Shrubb
1 cup lemon juice
1 cup All-Weather Grenadine (page 64)
½ cup Ginger Syrup (page 51)
Three 750-milliliter bottles good sparkling wine
2 bottles soda water (three-quarters of a 2-liter bottle)

Combine the Sicilian Shrubb, lemon juice, grenadine, and ginger syrup; allow the ingredients to marry for a bit.

Add sparkling wine and soda water at party time.

VARIATIONS:

- Adjust sweetness and strength by adding and subtracting simple syrup and soda water.

～ Nocino ～

Nocino, Italian for walnut, has deep roots in amaro, or Italian bitter liqueurs. Walnut was traditionally used as a digestive. Forget what you know about the realm of Frangelico, Kahlúa, and other coffee accompaniments; making these liqueurs yourself gets you closer to godliness. Nothing illustrates it better than this walnut number. The DIY advantage here lies in using the best ingredients (try to use organic walnuts) and the exact amount of sweet and spice that you like. Use in coffee, add a dash to whiskey, or sip straight. Nocino can also be used in desserts like soaked cakes and baba, chocolate truffles, and sweet sauces.

Makes 3 cups

2½ cups good-quality brandy
1½ cups walnuts, roughly chopped
1 teaspoon cardamom seeds, lightly crushed
½ vanilla bean, seeded or 1 teaspoon good vanilla extract
½ cup Simple Syrup (page 47), plus additional

Combine the brandy, walnuts, and cardamom seeds in at least a 24-ounce sterilized jar. Place the jar in a cool, dry spot for 1 week to 10 days, agitating every other day.

Add the vanilla bean and ½ cup simple syrup. Keep in the jar for 1 week to 10 days, shaking daily.

Strain the liqueur through a coffee filter, which is much slower but will remove all the nut dust. Repeat the straining until you're satisfied with clarity. Adjust for sweetness, if needed.

Divvy up the liqueur into small, sterilized, airtight bottles for gifts or one larger sterilized airtight bottle for storage. To let the flavors really marry, wait a few days before serving.

Use with your favorite brown liqueur, starting with a ratio of 2:1, brown to nocino.

- Use Honey or Light Molasses Simple Syrup (page 47). Both will add depth, and the bitterness in molasses marries very well with the flavors in coffee.

BRANDY STOUT

This drink manages to taste creamy without any dairy, thanks to the fine mousse of the stout.

1½ ounces brandy
1 ounce Nocino
1½ ounces stout

Combine the brandy, nocino, and stout in a pint glass with ice. Shake and strain into a rocks glass, rocks optional.

∿ Citrus Bitters ∿

Bottles of orange bitters lurk commonly enough amongst the sundries in the supermarket. Commercially produced citrus bitters just can't pack the sunshine wallop of the homemade variety. When dealing with anything fresh, the closer to the source, the better. The following recipe is a stellar changeup from the usual and just right when added to a gimlet or any lime-based cocktail. Also, I have a lime bias. Try it in "perfect" drinks. (A "perfect" drink refers to using half sweet and half dry vermouth in any cocktail that calls for either just one or the other.) You can adjust this recipe by substituting your favorite citrus, as well as modify the spice.

Makes 2 cups

2-inch section of lemongrass stalk, minced
½ teaspoon coriander
1 teaspoon grains of paradise
4 basil leaves
Zest of 6 limes
1½ cups high-proof vodka (100-proof or higher)
½ teaspoon gentian root

Lightly crush the lemongrass, coriander, and grains of paradise in a mortar and pestle; add the basil and bruise. Combine in a sterilized jar with the zest and vodka. Let the mixture macerate for 1 week to 10 days, shaking daily.

Add the gentian root and let the mixture marry for 1 week, shaking daily.

Double strain the mixture into a sterilized, airtight jar and store at room temperature away from heat and light.

GREEN GIN

A pink gin is the simple combination of gin and bitters, a merrie olde
English way of enjoying gin. This one … is green.

    2 ounces gin
    4 dashes Citrus Bitters, using the lime variation above
    1 thin slice lime peel

Stir the gin and bitters over ice and strain into a cocktail glass. Garnish
with the lime peel or wheel.

ᨑ Homemade Tonic ᨑ

Parents can lobby against high-fructose corn syrup for their children; I do it for my gin and tonic. Once you've had good tonic, you'll never let your gin suffer the 2-liter bottle or gun again, both lousy with HFCS and its tongue-coating or numbing effects. This recipe is an easy syrup used for mixing with soda water or aggressively sparkling water, giving gin the snappy mate it deserves. I've been burned sourcing *cinchona* bark, but I always love the stuff I get from the legend in the herbal scene, Tenzing Momo (page 6).

Makes 2 cups

4 cups water
2½ cups or more sugar
½ cup (about 2 stalks) finely chopped lemongrass
Zest and juice of 2 limes, divided
3 tablespoons powdered cinchona bark
3 tablespoons citric acid
1 teaspoon juniper berries
½ teaspoon peppercorns

Bring the water to a boil in a heavy-bottom saucepan. Add the sugar to taste, stir until dissolved, and reduce the heat to medium-low.

Add the lemongrass, lime zest, cinchona bark, citric acid, juniper berries, and peppercorns. Simmer for 30 minutes.

Remove from the heat and let cool. Double strain the mixture, add the lime juice, and keep in a sterilized airtight jar or bottle in the refrigerator for up to 6 weeks.

VARIATIONS:

- You can also mix it with distilled water and carbonate the entire thing if you possess a soda siphon or a fancy soda-making machine.
- Experiment with spices based on your favorite gin.

GIN & HOMEMADE TONIC

I feel weird including an actual recipe for this ubiquitous highball, but since there's some assembly required...

1½ ounces gin
1 ounce Homemade Tonic
4 ounces soda water
1 lime wedge

Combine the gin and tonic in a rocks glass, add ice, and top with the soda—as little or as much as you like. Stir and garnish with a lime wedge.

ᴧ Vodka Soup ᴧ

I had many long arguments regarding the proper season for a Bloody Mary. It's my book so I won, but this recipe takes the Bloody Mary to another level and therefore deserves honorable mention. And, according to my friend Lisa Simpson, who developed it, "It's exactly what you need when you're stuck on a chairlift with a bunch of pre-Sundance douchebags in Deer Valley."

Makes eight 6-ounce servings, or 2 servings plus 1 thermos

3 cups beef broth
1 cup tomato juice
1½ teaspoons microplaned onion
½ teaspoon freshly cracked black pepper
1 big splash Worcestershire sauce
4 tablespoons lemon juice
8 ounces or more vodka
Salt

Simmer the broth, tomato juice, onion, black pepper, and Worcestershire sauce in a non-aluminum saucepan for a few minutes. (Aluminum will produce off-flavors, and if it boils or simmers too long it makes the tomato juice taste weird.)

Add the lemon juice and the vodka to taste; stir for a few more minutes. Remove from the heat and add the salt to taste. Serve warm.

～ Spring ～

DRY WHITE VERMOUTH

PANDAN LEAF INFUSION
Martini Envy

FRUIT (AND PRODUCE) LIQUEUR
The Sour

CHAMOMILE LIQUEUR
The Betty White

CELERY BITTERS
The Harry Carey

RHUBARB BITTERS
Basic Hot Toddy

INFUSED VINEGAR
Mr. Knickerbocker

RED PEPPER TINCTURE
Michelada

∽ Dry White Vermouth ∽

The advent of the very dry, "don't even let it see the vermouth bottle" vodka martini has managed to malign vermouth for years. This shirking was aided and abetted by bars that put the same bottle of crappy dry and sweet vermouth in the well every night, never dated for freshness, never tasted to see if it was even still palatable. We call this period the '90s.

Vermouth, quite simply, is wine that's been fortified and loaded with herbs and spices.

Dry, or white, vermouth—the kind that goes in a martini—may also be described as French in recipes, especially older cocktail books. Dry vermouth typically appeals to those who like their very dry white wines or gin and tonics because they are very herbal, as a rule, with a sharp finish.

Red, or sweet, vermouth—the kind that goes in a manhattan—may also be described as Italian in recipes. Its flavor can range anywhere from spicy sangria with a kick to something as complex as a young, still half-red tawny port.

Blanc (or *bianco*) vermouth—the kind normally drunk on the rocks—is not as heavy in the mouth as the popular Lillet, but it delivers a lightly sweet liquid oozing intense spicy aromas and flavors.

To make vermouth, you mull wine, add herbs and spices, and dose it with alcohol. Whether you start with cheap or older wine, don't use anything you wouldn't drink by itself. It only lowers the potential outcome.

Makes 4 cups

1 teaspoon coriander
½ teaspoon chamomile
½ teaspoon fennel seed
½ teaspoon nigella seed
4 to 6 fresh sage leaves, or 1 teaspoon dried sage
1 allspice berry
Zest of ½ orange
Zest of 1 lemon
½ teaspoon gentian root
3 tablespoons vodka, gin, or grappa
4 cups (1 bottle) driest white wine

Lightly crush the coriander, chamomile, fennel seed, nigella seed, sage leaves, allspice berry, and orange and lemon zest in a mortar and pestle. Combine the mixture with the gentian root, vodka, and wine in a medium heavy-bottom saucepan; bring to a boil.

Boil for 5 minutes; lower the heat and simmer for 15 minutes. Remove from the heat and let cool.

Transfer the mixture to a large jar, seal, and let sit overnight or up to 24 hours.

Strain the mixture into an appropriately sized, sterilized jar or bottle and refrigerate for up to 4 weeks.

VARIATIONS:

- To make a slightly off-dry vermouth, double the orange peel, substitute ¾ cup plus 2 tablespoons amontillado sherry for the wine, and add 2 tablespoons simple syrup, which will both sweeten and add a richer mouthfeel.

- For sweet or red vermouth, use a dry, light red wine with little tannin, and substitute cream sherry or sweet marsala for a portion of the wine.

∿ Pandan Leaf Infusion ∿

That Saran Wrap slice of bright green cake in the Asian market may scream fake, but it's more likely flavored with pandan leaf. Used in Southeast Asian cooking both savory and sweet, pandan gives off a vaguely vanilla aroma with a faint fennel edge. This naturally green concoction can be put to fun use without disgustingly fake or minty results (I'm talking about you, Midori and crème de menthe). Use in cocktail recipes to replace vanilla, vodka, or lighter, fruitier gins for a softer, slightly herbal result. It's a dynamite replacement for vodka in a vesper or a gimlet.

Makes 3 cups

4 pandan leaves, torn into strips
3 cups vodka, 80 proof

Combine the leaves and vodka in a jar and let macerate for 1 to 2 weeks.

Remove leaves, strain, and keep in a sterlized jar or bottle at room temperature. Infusion will keep indefinitely.

MARTINI ENVY

Though on its own it has some sweetness, the Pandan Leaf Infusion changes the pace from the average vodka or gin in many drink recipes, including an almost-classic martini.

2 ounces Pandan Leaf Infusion
½ ounce homemade or good-quality vermouth
Dash Celery Bitters (page 143)
Lemon twist (optional)

Combine the infusion, vermouth, and bitters with ice and stir; strain into some sort of cocktail glass.

Garnish with a lemon twist.

⁓ Fruit (and Produce) Liqueur ⁓

To make the majority of fruit liqueurs, fresh or dried fruit macerates with alcohol to extract the goods of the skins and comingle with the fruit's juices. The basic rule to any recipe using fruit: use the freshest fruit in the highest proof alcohol and adjust accordingly with simple syrup. Simple syrup also helps in diluting the alcohol strength.

Time may be the most complicated ingredient in any infusion, especially those involving fresh fruit and produce. Sink the fruit in alcohol for a few weeks, strain, and add simple syrup and/or dilute to suit your purposes. For timing I follow the rule that the more delicate the fruit, the faster the extraction. I use the ugly factor to determine doneness: if the fruit looks like the life has been sucked out of it, it has.

Plug in and play with the following recipe at will. Quantities are just guidelines, but keep in mind the strength of an ingredient, whether it's tart or bitter or pungent. If you want a liquor instead of a liqueur, reduce the simple syrup to 2 tablespoons and add 1 teaspoon at a time, to your taste.

Makes 3 cups

USE THIS BASIC RATIO
1 cup fruit
¼ to ½ cup Simple Syrup (page 47)
2½ cups 80-proof or higher liquor (vodka, gin, rum, tequila, etc.)
2 teaspoons spice (optional)
¼ cup fresh herb (optional)
Zest of 2 lemons or limes, or other citrus (optional)

Clean the fruit; if necessary, break down into pieces (quarters of plum, chunks of melon, slices of fennel, strips of zest, etc.).

Combine the fruit and simple syrup with the liquor in a large jar and macerate for 2 weeks.

You want the alcohol to leech the color, aromatics, and as much of the volatile compounds from whatever you put in it. So the best clue to readiness, then, is the fruit itself. After one week, how does it look? Check for color and general attractiveness. The more delicate the fruit, the faster the infusion.

Double strain the mixture and keep in a sterilized, airtight jar or bottle.

THE SOUR

The sour is the genesis of many cocktails—the daiquiri, margarita, and sidecar, for example.

One of the most bastardized of classic cocktails, this drink was murdered by wedding bartenders in the 1980s, most of whom threw a jigger of whiskey over ice, squirted some neon sour mix on top, threw in a cherry, and called it a day. This was a time when bartenders got sloppy. The real thing is completely different. You can make these drinks without the egg white. But—would you give someone cake without the frosting? See page 151 for more info on using egg whites in drinks.

2 ounces spirit
1 ounce lemon juice
1 teaspoon Simple Syrup (page 47)
1 egg white (see page 151)
Flavored bitters (see page 60) (optional)

Combine the spirit, lemon juice, simple syrup, egg white, and bitters in a shaker without ice. Add the spring from a Hawthorne strainer (see page 34) and shake like crazy. Remove the spring, add ice, and shake vigorously again.

Strain into a cocktail or coupe glass.

VARIATIONS:

- Give the foam a light drizzle of bitters.

- Substitute lime juice for lemon juice, especially for white liquors.

- Ten sours to try beyond whiskey: Your own liquor/liqueur infusion (page 41), pisco (page 40), rum, gin, tequila, brandy, fruit brandy, Metaxa, Strega, or a dark semisweet sherry sour (try oloroso).

- Add your favorite fruit bitters or flavored syrup for depth.

- Sprinkle the top with Finishing Sugar (page 54).

The Original: Pisco Sour

This South American brandy's "official drink" status is a huge bone of contention between Chileans and Peruvians. Both countries make the spirit, a clear or soft amber color depending on whether it never sees oak or spends only a little time in barrels. Peru claims it made it first. From grapes like moscatel (a variant of the Muscat grape) that are usually turned into sweet wines, pisco ends up having a hint of grape (like grappa) as well as a tiny sweet note without any actual sweetness, much as rum has that residual sugar-cane aroma and flavor. However, clear pisco has a sophisticated edge over white rum, with nuance galore.

I've learned over the years that certain drinks register as a slam-dunk. When bored or adventurous bar patrons leave their pick of poison up to me, I whip out the tart, creamy Pisco Sour.

Duggan McDonnell, owner of Cantina bar in San Francisco, explains this drink's connection to the West Coast . . . of North America. "The Pisco Sour is not just the national cocktail of Peru. Victor Morris, a native of the Bay Area and an American expat who had a bar in Lima, popularized the Pisco Sour in the 1920s as a variation on the whiskey sour. Within a decade, Pisco's fame had reached as far north as San Francisco, where it became popular after Prohibition ended. Pisco had already been popular here since the Gold Rush, and Pisco Punch was all the rage before Prohibition."

McDonnel has done more than champion Pisco's comeback; he is the co-owner and blender of Campo de Encanto Pisco. "Good-quality Pisco is one of the world's oldest distillates. It's single distilled from the grape, without any bells and whistles or barrel aging and is often blended, like Scotch. And just like Scotch or wine, Pisco is capable of capturing a sense of place. We haven't really seen in this country all that Pisco can offer."

⤳ Chamomile Liqueur ⤳

Forget whether or not you like chamomile tea; it's akin to lowly shake for this recipe. The good stuff, nothing but flowers, smells like rolling in daisies strewn on wet hay. Use the freshest dried chamomile flowers you can find from either an herbalist or a spice merchant.

This liqueur came out of a conversation with Andrew Friedman and Keith Waldbauer, co-owners of Liberty Bar in Seattle (517 15th Avenue East). Nowhere else in Seattle combines pristine drinks with such an accommodating attitude and a splash of irreverence as Liberty, a small bar in the Capitol Hill neighborhood. Andrew just told me about the white dog drink he made with a chamomile grappa liqueur, lemon bitters, and white dog, saying it was the first white dog drink he'd ever loved. That put the chamomile bee in my bonnet.

Makes 3 cups

1½ cups chamomile flowers, highest quality
2¼ cups vodka, at least 80 proof
1 cup Lemon Coriander Syrup (see Citrus Syrup recipe, page 50)

Combine the chamomile flowers and vodka, seal, and agitate daily for 4 days.

Strain out the flowers, add the syrup. Strain again and transfer to a sterilized jar or bottle. This liqueur keeps for months, but after two months, its delicate edges will start to fade.

THE BETTY WHITE

After I made the liqueur, I didn't know what to do with it. I still make concoctions that never see the light of day. My friend Jay Kuehner, after drinking the liqueur, said, "This reminds me of all those Northern Italian herbal liqueurs, those things you love so much, like your beloved Strega," he said. "I'd keep it as simple as possible so you don't lose any of the chamomile. Most people drink chamomile tea with lemon, so just do that."

Sometimes, I make things I don't really want to put in a cocktail. This liqueur is so pretty on its own, it doesn't need making up. Keep It Simple Stupid, a cliché for a reason. Even chefs and bartenders can forget this. Jay, Andrew, and Keith don't know that they helped make this liqueur and the drink below, but they did. And so it goes with most cocktail lists. The high-octane version of a treasured Celestial Seasonings favorite, I call this drink The Betty White because it's a sassy take on a traditional cocktail, the White Lady (gin, cointreau, and lemon).

1½ ounces mild gin, like Beefeater
¾ ounce Chamomile Liqueur
¼ ounce lemon juice
A float of bubbly (optional)

Combine the gin, liqueur, and lemon juice in a shaker with ice. Shake and strain into a pretty glass. Top with a pinkie's worth of bubbles, if you like. If it's too tart, you can add a little simple syrup.

∿ Celery Bitters ∿

I love celery bitters because it knocks the sweet off the top of a rye whiskey drink, reinforcing a savory note similar to rye bread. Likewise, it adds depth to the simple martini or a Pimm's cup (it's a natural match for the latter).

Celery bitters fell off the cocktail map for tens of years. This recipe follows the traditional vein of celery bitters and the flavor it is meant to impart, as interpreted with an assist from Karyn Schwartz of Sugarpill in the Capitol Hill neighborhood of Seattle. Fresh dandelion makes it outrageous. (Yes, we still have weeds in the winter in the Northwest.)

Makes 2 cups

¼ cup dandelion leaves and heads
10 medium fresh mint leaves
⅓ cup celery seed
2 teaspoons coriander seeds
1 pinch cumin seed
1 allspice berry
2 cups 100-proof or higher whiskey or rum

Lightly crush the dandelion, mint, celery seed, coriander seeds, cumin seed, and allspice berry in a mortar and pestle. Combine with the whiskey and store in a jar for 10 days to 2 weeks, shaking daily.

Double strain the mixture into small, sterilized jars and store at room temperature. It will keep for a few months. For ease of use in your bar, transfer into small 2- or 4-ounce bottles that have eyedropper caps (see Resources, page 186).

THE HARRY CAREY

This drink is so named because every flavor it possesses can be found in a Chicago-style hot dog, highly recommended as a baseball opening day mojo-bringer. (Uh… no guarantees for Cubs fans.)

    2 ounces Savory Akvavit (page 112)
    1 bar spoon pickle juice, preferably sweet-and-sour
    2 dashes Celery Bitters
    Lemon twist or pickle slice (optional)

Combine the akvavit, pickle juice, and bitters with ice and stir; strain into some sort of cocktail glass.

Garnish with a lemon twist or pickle slice. Toast to the "holy cow" before drinking.

VARIATIONS:

- Add ½ ounce Red Pepper Tincture (page 149) or 2 ounces tomato juice for a strong alternative to a Bloody Mary.

◠ Rhubarb Bitters ◠

I almost fought for a fifth season just for this weird vegetable we treat like a fruit. The raw stalks are plenty tart, the backbone of the flavor you achieve when cooking rhubarb for pies and sweets. This bitter livens up any drink with a dominant citrus note, and it's the only deviant thing about my Sazeracs (the official cocktail of New Orleans), when I leave NOLA's beloved Peychaud's bitters behind.

Never use the leaves, which are toxic. You can sweeten with simple syrup or herbal syrup to really drive it home.

My actual, more complicated version of this recipe appears in *Bitters: A Spirited History of a Classic Cure-all, With Cocktails, Recipes, and Formulas* by Brad Thomas Parsons (Ten Speed Press).

Makes about 2 cups

1 teaspoon grains of paradise
1 teaspoon nigella seeds
½ teaspoon coriander seeds
1½ cups diced fresh rhubarb
Zest of 1 medium orange
2 cups vodka
½ teaspoon gentian root
1 teaspoon sassafras
2 tablespoons Simple Syrup or Herbal Syrup (pages 47 and 49)

Lightly crush the grains of paradise, nigella seeds, and coriander seeds and combine with the rhubarb, zest, and vodka in a large jar. Seal and store in a cool, dry place for 2 weeks, shaking daily.

After 2 weeks, add the gentian root and sassafras and store for another 2 weeks, shaking every few days.

Double strain into a sterilized, airtight jar, add simple syrup to taste, and store at room temperature. Use within six months. For ease of use or to gift, pour into 2- or 4-ounce apothecary bottles with eyedroppers for tops. Use rhubarb bitters as a sub for any bitters in cocktails with a fruit element or citrus base. It is also incredible in a simple gin and tonic.

BASIC HOT TODDY

This isn't so much a recipe as it is a pep talk. No other drink you order at the bar can go so horribly wrong or sideways as a hot toddy. Hot toddies fail because either the customer has a certain unexpressed expectation, or the bartender doesn't give a rip. The root recipe calls for whiskey, hot water, and lemon. That's it. This recipe offers several options for increased soothing.

1½ ounces brown liquor
½ ounce liqueur or Simple Syrup (page 47) (optional)
1 dash orange or spiced bitters (page 127) (optional)
4½ ounces hot, mild liquid—water, tea, lemonade
Lemon to taste

Combine liquor, liqueur, and bitters in your glass and pour the hot liquid over. Garnish with lemon or add lemon juice to taste.

VARIATIONS:

• Add 1 tablespoon butter (better if it's spiced) and you have a hot buttered … something.

∼ Infused Vinegar ∼

The fun starts here. This recipe has every chance to change the way you make cocktails, and also salad. Start with a simple, bright, and tangy fruit like pineapple or nectarine.

Makes about 1 cup

BASE
1 cup light vinegar such as white wine, rice, or champagne
⅓ cup sugar

ANY ONE OR A COMBINATION OF THE FOLLOWING
⅔ cup fruit or veggies, appropriately sliced or diced small
1 to 2 tablespoons whole spice
¼ cup fresh herbs, packed
Zest of 1 to 2 citrus pieces

The long way (slower maceration gives the drinking vinegar a more complex flavor):

Combine the vinegar with whatever flavoring you're adding and let it macerate in a jar for up to 10 days. Strain the mixture well. Bring the now-flavored vinegar to a boil in a saucepan. Add sugar and let boil for five more minutes.

Remove from the heat, let the mixture cool, double strain, and transfer it into a sterilized jar.

The short way (because sometimes you want it now):

Bring the vinegar, sugar, and what you're infusing to a boil and boil for 5 minutes. Turn down the heat and simmer for up to 20 minutes.

Remove from the heat, let the mixture cool, double strain and transfer it into a sterilized, airtight jar.

MR. KNICKERBOCKER

This is a take on an unremarkable recipe from the *Joy of Cooking*. The original included rum, lemon juice, and both raspberry and pineapple syrups, making a sweet, liquor-heavy cocktail. This version is lighter and uses pineapple juice that creates a layer of froth when shaken with ice. The vinegar ups the quench quotient and cuts the rum's sweetness.

1½ ounces darker rum
1 ounce pineapple juice
½ ounce lemon juice
½ recipe All-Weather Grenadine or fruit acid (pages 64 and 170)
1 bar spoon pineapple vinegar

Pour the rum, pineapple juice, lemon juice, grenadine, and pineapple vinegar into a chilled pint glass. Add ice, shake, and strain into a highball glass prepacked with ice.

VARIATIONS:

- A bit more pineapple juice makes Mr. K. a long drink that's breakfast worthy.

- Add an egg white to make it a Mrs. K. (see page 151).

⌒ Red Pepper Tincture ⌒

What to call this . . . ? It's not a purée. Though you could add red pepper purée to the mix and have a dynamite take on the Bloody Mary, but that's a ton of peppers. This is far more intense—a shot in the arm for a gin gimlet or tequila, and a little vitamin C to tide you over until things start sprouting from the ground. Thin it out a bit with lime juice and water for a take on sangrita (the little shooter that accompanies a shot of tequila in some circles). Special equipment needed: blender, finest mesh strainer.

Makes 1 cup

4 red bell peppers
½ jalapeño pepper, seeded and minced
12 cilantro leaves, finely chopped
½ teaspoon freshly ground coriander seed
1 cup vodka

Char the bell peppers under the broiler or over a gas flame, making sure to blacken all sides. When cool, remove the skins and dice the flesh, discarding the skins and innards.

Combine the bell peppers, jalapeño, cilantro leaves, coriander seed, and vodka in a wide-mouth jar and let macerate for 1 week, shaking daily.

In a blender, purée the mixture and refrigerate in an airtight jar. Use within 2 weeks for optimum taste.

VARIATIONS:

- You can modify the heat with hot sauce, if you don't have fresh jalapeño, and substitute spices—cumin, for example. Use tequila instead of vodka if you're planning to serve with tequila.

MICHELADA

This beer cocktail can mean anything from lime and salt in beer to pepper sauce and more ingredients than a Bloody Mary, depending on where you order one. This version takes a cue from the Midwestern red beer (cheap lager and tomato juice).

2 sprigs of cilantro
2 to 4 lime wedges
Salt (optional)
1 ounce Red Pepper Tincture
1 bottle or can of Mexican beer (or light lager, such as pilsner)

In a pint glass, muddle the cilantro and lime with salt. Add the tincture and fill the glass halfway with beer. Stir and pack with ice. Drink, adding the rest of the beer in succession as you drink it down.

On Foam and Using Egg Whites

You might think using egg whites in your drink is gross or unsanitary, but do you wash your eggs before you crack them for a scramble? No? That's gross. Accidentally dipping your nose into a layer of thick creamy foam on its way to meringue? That's not gross. That's heaven, or at least cloud nine.

In Seattle, restaurants have to put a disclaimer on all menus, reading "eating raw or undercooked foods may cause food-borne illness." The truth is, people freak out about raw eggs and salmonella, and that's a personal choice. You can always use pasteurized egg whites if you want, or even reconstituted powdered egg whites. Getting salmonella from a raw egg is very rare and likely to happen because of something that was on the shell, not inside.

Proper cracking: Wash all eggs before using. Crack eggs one at a time, splitting rather than collapsing the shell into the egg. Capture the yolk in one hand while letting the white run free into a tiny bowl. Only use what slips through your fingers naturally, discarding the little sack within the white of the egg—you don't want that to ruin the texture. Check for shells and then it's ready to add to the cocktail.

Proper shaking: Build all the components of your drink in a mixing glass without ice. Remove the spring of a Hawthorne strainer (see page 34) and toss that in, too. Cover with a tin and shake vigorously for 45 seconds. Crack the tin, add ice, and then shake for up to one minute more. Strain into a coupe glass or something fun and fitting. Drink to soothe your aching arms.

Powdered egg white: Reconstituted, these are a perfectly acceptable substitute for the freshies, and for the germaphobe.

A vegan moment: Though it will certainly change the flavor of a cocktail, when you add both pineapple juice and a few dashes of bitters to a drink and shake, you will produce a good-looking foam, not as finely moussed as an egg white but nice. Just adjust a cocktail's other sweet components to make way for the very sweet pineapple.

~ Summer ~

WHITE SANGRIA

PICNIC GIN

SUGAR CANE–INFUSED RUM
Caipirinha

COCONUT RUM
6-Word Daiquiri

HIBISCUS & SPICE–INFUSED TEQUILA
Perro Salado

MINTED RUM
Mojito, Redux

SPICED LIQUOR
Horchata Borracha

FALERNUM
Corn & Oil

BERRY ACID
Slow Gin Fizz

CHERRY BITTERS
Whiskey Soda, Fashioned

FRUIT PURÉE
Bellini

BITTER LEMON SODA

<YOUR TOWN HERE> LEMONADE

～ White Sangria ～

The great sangria myth says that you make sangria out of cheap red wine to make it taste better. Correction: Historically, that's the definition of mulled wine. Sangria is a light punch meant to be fun, a way to drink red wine as refreshment. But like most anything else, the ingredients of sangria determine its worthiness. I started making white wine sangria only because a good, cheap white wine is not as hard to find. The key to good sangria is just to wing it. Start with this basic recipe and make it your own—use Cointreau instead of brandy, add Spice Syrup (page 50). This recipe can just as easily be made with red wine, but the color fruit and hibiscus give to the white wine is so cool.

Makes twelve 6-ounce servings

1 cup water
1 cup Simple Syrup (page 47)
Zest and juice of 4 to 6 oranges, divided
2 tablespoons coriander seed
1 tablespoon hibiscus flowers
1 tablespoon lavender
Fruit for floating (plum, apricot, nectarine, citrus)
1 cup brandy
6 cups (2 bottles) dry white wine

Bring the water and simple syrup to a boil in a saucepan. Add the zest, coriander seed, hibiscus flowers, and lavender. Reduce the heat to simmer and steep for 20 minutes or until the mixture is reduced by half.

Meanwhile, slice and throw the fruit into a large punch bowl, preferably, or a gallon jar (half-gallon will cut it too close). Add the brandy, wine, and orange juice.

Remove the syrup mixture from the heat and let cool. Strain and mix into the wine and fruit salad.

Sangria will keep for up to 4 days in the fridge.

TO SERVE

Chill for serving or serve over ice.

VARIATIONS:

- Add sparkling wine or cider, or seltzer for effervescence. (Sugary sodas are sangria's Public Enemy #1.)

ᨆ Picnic Gin ᨆ

The genesis of this recipe is a kind of tub gin, not the kind associated with Prohibition but rather with college, a ton of cut fruit, and a tub in which to soak it in whatever heinous alcohol is lying around. Hairy buffalo or spodie—that's what we called it, anyway. It's not that the idea lacks legs, just focus. Fruit soaked in booze is a gorgeous idea. Here's a take on spodie, inspired by its garnish. One serving of this recipe is as strong as a martini.

Makes about 5 cups

3 cups gin (or vodka infusion or Akvavit) (page 111)
3 cups watermelon, cubed
½ cup Falernum (page 168)

In a large jar, combine the gin and watermelon. Let macerate for 2 days.

Strain the liquid, pressing the watermelon and pushing as much liquid and juice through as possible. Add up to ½ cup of falernum, to taste. Mixture will keep up to a week in the fridge.

TO SERVE

Serve in 3-ounce portions over ice.

⤳ Sugar Cane–Infused Rum ⤶

The majority of rum is distilled from the by-products left from the various steps of extracting sugar from the sugar cane. A few finer rums—specifically *rhum agricole*—are distilled from the freshly pressed cane juice itself. Cane juice tastes like a grassy or leafy sweetened rice milk, with a little of the flavor of condensed milk. It adds a depth to the telltale sweetness of aged or darker rum, and comes off best in a simple cocktail (read: nothing tiki).

Makes 3 cups

1 cup fresh sugar cane, chopped
3 cups good-quality rum

In a large, sterilized jar, combine the sugar cane and rum. Seal and store in a cool, dry place for 2 to 4 weeks.

Strain the rum into a sterilized, airtight bottle. Use in any simple rum-based drink, ideally a mostly spirituous one.

VARIATIONS:

- Try this recipe with cachaça—fermented sugar cane liquor from Brazil—to elevate a Caipirinha (below).

CAIPIRINHA

Somewhere between a gimlet and an old-fashioned . . . the caipirinha is the national cocktail of Brazil.

4 to 6 lime quarters
2 teaspoons sugar
2 ounces sugar cane–infused cachaça

Muddle, or lightly press, the limes and sugar together in a rocks glass. Add ice and cachaça, then stir.

To better incorporate the ingredients, dump the entire drink into a mixing glass and then back into the rocks glass.

THE GARDE MANGER

I've made my own coconut rum, but I got the idea for using sugar cane from Jay Kuehner, who has bartended for as long as I have but really found his stride during his stint lording over the walk-in-closet-size bar at Sambar, which resides in a strange, in-between neighborhood of Seattle, one canal north of downtown. He was giving a drinking lesson at the bar of the Sorrento Hotel and sent me to the International District for fresh sugar cane juice. (Ever had it? It magically cures even the worst hangovers.)

My metaphor about making drinks being similar to making salad dressing comes from Jay. I can't remember ever ordering a specific cocktail at his bar; I just drink what he makes for me after he asks a few questions to gauge my mood. It's worth it to see what captures his mood, for in addition to the cocktails listed on the menu, Jay just wings it. Granted, his winging is based on a deep knowledge of drink recipes and what he has fresh on hand. He treats his bar a little bit like a chef would treat the pantry—starting with the basics and adding or modifying with a little of this and a little of that.

On a recent visit, he had mellow chile water and was really into tequila. He mixed these with fresh orange juice, mint syrup (I think), and a little amber amaro and god knows what else to make a drink. It tasted nothing and everything like that which was in it, and I loved it.

The thing I learned was the merit of forgetting, of making a great drink with a certain ingredient and then forgetting about it the next weekend and making something else.

Because really, it's never the last drink you're ever going to have. Until it is.

Sambar
425 NW Market Street
Seattle's Fremont/Ballard neighborhood
www.sambarseattle.com

⚭ Coconut Rum ⚭

Let's just take store-brought coconut rum off the table, for if you can't say anything nice . . . Macerating real coconut in rum gives it a fresh, naturally sweet edge and fantastic body. Forget any ideas of suntan lotion here.

Makes 3 cups

1 whole coconut
3 cups good-quality rum
½ vanilla bean, halved and seeded, ½ teaspoon peppercorns, or ½
   teaspoon grains of paradise (optional)

Without losing a finger, break down the coconut and separate out the meat. Reserve the juice for breakfast or for other cocktails.

In a large, sterilized jar (for easier egress), combine the coconut meat, rum, and the optional ingredient you choose. Seal and store in a cool, dry place for 2 to 3 weeks.

Strain the rum and keep in a sterilized, airtight jar or bottle. Use in any simple rum-based drink, especially daiquiris.

Variations:

- You could put the lime in the coconut, so to speak, by adding 10 makrut lime leaves to this recipe for added flavor and an insane aroma.

6-WORD DAIQUIRI

The title of this drink references the best thing Hemingway, the greatest American drinker, ever wrote ("For sale: Baby shoes, never worn."), because this drink was inspired by not having the ingredients to make a Hemingway Daiquiri one very late, hot night.

2 ounces flavored rum
¾ ounce lime juice
½ ounce lime or orange Cello (page 117) or orange liqueur
1 splash Simple Syrup (page 47)
1 egg white (see page 151)
Cherry Bitters (page 172)

Combine the rum, lime juice, cello, simple syrup to taste, and egg white into a shaker with the spring of a Hawthorne strainer (see page 34). Shake like hell; add ice and shake again.

Strain into a cocktail or up glass. Dash or drizzle the bitters over the foamy top.

◥ Hibiscus & Spice–Infused Tequila ◢

Tequila gets a bad reputation mostly because it is one of the go-to beverages for those using *party* as a verb. If you won't sip a shot of tequila straight anymore, try this one. All the ingredients make for an incredibly fast infusion, one that still lets tequila's earth nature shine through while adding tang, spice, and citrus. Think of it as a *muy macho aperitivo*. Rebuild the margarita with it; serve it straight or on the rocks with coconut water.

Makes 3 cups

> 3 cups good-quality reposado tequila (see page 39)
> 3 tablespoons dried hibiscus flowers
> Zest of 1 orange
> ½ jalapeño pepper, sliced and seeded
> 3-inch chunk lemongrass, chopped

Pour the tequila into a large, sterilized jar. Add the hibiscus and shake occasionally. After 1 hour strain out the flowers or the infusion will be overly tangy.

Combine the now-red tequila with the zest, pepper, and lemongrass; let macerate in a cool spot for 4 days. Strain and store in a sterilized, airtight jar or bottle at room temperature.

PERRO SALADO

This recipe is an alternative for a Salty Dog (which uses vodka), a standard highball.

> Kosher salt
> 1½ ounce Hibiscus & Spice–Infused Tequila
> 3 to 4 ounces fresh grapefruit juice

Rim a rocks glass with the salt, fill with ice, and add the tequila and grapefruit juice.

∼ Minted Rum ∼

Fact #1: Right now I run a restaurant across the street from a beach. A beach in Seattle, but still. Fact #2: I hate mojitos. This recipe comes from the need to reconcile these two facts. In Phase One of my Operation Mojito for summer, I use the same logic for seasoning both sides of a steak: if the objective of a mojito is a hit of mint, get mint into as many components of the drink as possible to assure you never suffer a flaccid, watered-down, slightly flavored rum and soda again. Get your hands on some Moroccan mint if you can; it has the perfect balance of perfume and pungency for cocktails.

Makes 3 cups

2 cups lightly packed mint sprigs
3 cups good-quality rum (never white, never while)
4-inch portion of lemongrass stalk, roughly chopped

Bruise the mint in the bottom of a large, sterilized jar, which will expose a bit more of the oils at the start. Add the rum and lemongrass and let the mixture sit for 1 week, agitating it daily.

Strain and store in a sterilized, airtight jar or bottle at room temperature for up to 2 months, but that shouldn't be necessary when you discover phase two....

MOJITO, REDUX

The mojito is a fine drink . . . at your house. In the bar it is often abused and misused, and even when made correctly makes a heck of a mess. It also has a way of maintaining deliciousness for only the first few sips, then completely failing to satisfy for the last half of the drink, as if the ice melts three times too fast. Limes and mint muddled with a little sugar, ice, rum, and soda water—that's a mojito. Here it is again, now with 75 percent more mint. This recipe will ruin all other patio parties for your friends.

2 lime wedges
Mint sprig
½ ounce Mint-Lime Syrup (see Flavored Simple Syrup, page 49)
1½ ounces Minted Rum (page 163)
3 to 4 ounces soda water

In the bottom of a large rocks glass, muddle the lime, a few mint leaves, and syrup. (Reserve a leaf or a 2-leaf sprig for garnish.) You want to release a little mint oil, not make pesto.

Add ice and the rum, then top with the soda water to taste. Garnish with the remaining mint.

∼ Spiced Liquor ∼

This is something that's really difficult to write a recipe for because it's such a matter of personal taste, and much of the time I just lazily throw stuff in a jar with bourbon. Use the measurements as guidelines, and trade anything out for your favorite spice. This version not only makes an incredible Basic Hot Toddy (page 146), but it can go in Horchata Borracha (page 166) and will change up a manhattan (page 178).

Makes 3 cups

2 teaspoons cardamom
1 tablespoon grains of paradise
½ teaspoon fennel seed
½ tablespoon sugar
Zest of 1 medium orange
2 cinnamon sticks
3 cups whiskey (rye, bourbon, or your preferred)

In a mortar and pestle, lightly crush the cardamom, grains of paradise, fennel, and sugar.

In a jar, combine the sugar mixture with the zest, cinnamon sticks, and whiskey and let macerate for 3 weeks, shaking daily.

Double strain and keep the mixture in a sterilized, airtight jar or bottle.

HORCHATA BORRACHA

Creamy drinks get a bad rap because they're considered the mainstay of amateur drinkers. Bartenders have trust issues, but that doesn't mean creamy boozy drinks aren't good, just that in a bar they usually end up involving a mop. Yes, this recipe steals a page from the chai playbook, but no, I didn't want to use the phrase "high chai." Cardamom, star anise, and nutmeg...feel free to customize the spice to your style.

Consider this boozy version of a taco truck favorite the spicy alternative to the oh-so-trashy White Russian. It plays nice with spicy food. Horchata traditionally uses tiger nuts, but rice milk and cinnamon have become the default in this country.

Makes two 8-ounce servings

    1 cup water
    1 strong black tea bag
    3 cinnamon sticks
    1 teaspoon lightly ground cardamom
    1 cup almond milk (see Note)
    2 ounces brown liquor, preferably rum or spiced rum

In a small saucepan, heat the water to boiling and add the tea bag, cinnamon sticks, and cardamom. Lower the heat to medium and let the mixture reduce by about one-third. Remove the mixture from the heat; when cool, combine with the milk and liquor over ice (can be shaken first).

Note: Use soy at your own risk; its texture with alcohol is very...strange.

WHISKEY

Scotch, bourbon, and rye are all whiskeys: grain-distilled spirits that age for a time in oak barrels. These three major categories of whiskey are distinguished from one another by origin and ingredients. In America, rye was one of the most commonly used whiskey-making grains from the time of the signing of the Constitution (and even longer in eastern states). As spirits production spread west, distillers used a larger variety of grains to make their products—in Tennessee and Kentucky, the preference for corn begat bourbon—choosing other grains over rye sometimes for flavor and sometimes out of necessity.

Rye whiskey must be distilled from a mash containing at least 51 percent rye. This is not to be confused with Canadian whisky (no *e*), which is often referred to as "rye whisky" by our friends up north but which has not necessarily been made from the same amount of rye we require in the States. Rye should have a characteristic spicy, peppery note or zing; this spice is completely different from the sweeter aromas found in bourbon. Rye whiskey also gets the same slight bitterness from the grain you find in the aftertaste of a slice of dark rye bread. The flavor of rye whiskey is generally less sweet than that of bourbon.

ᴧ Falernum ᴧ

Falernum, a thick, sweet syrup used in tropical drinks, historically includes the dominant note of clove, along with ginger, lime, and sometimes almond.

Falernum is an argument against history, for here the old not necessarily being the good. If you grew up in the 1980s or '90s, chances are you're off cloves (from the ever-popular tobaccoless cigarettes), almost as much as you're off patchouli. This falernum takes the *idea* of the liqueur by using a few spices to add depth and ditching the clove for mace. Adjust the spices and simple syrup to taste. It's more interesting because it's fresh, not because of the exact measurements.

Use in a rum collins, rum and tonic, daiquiris, or any cocktail calling for falernum: zombie, rum swizzle, or the Royal Bermuda Cocktail, for example.

Makes 2½ cups

1½ cups good-quality rum (not white)
Zest of 7 large limes (a little bit of pith is OK)
1 tablespoon shredded gingerroot
1 tablespoon mace blades, lightly crushed
1 teaspoon grains of paradise, lightly crushed
2 to 4 whole star anise pieces, lightly crushed
¾ cup Simple Syrup (page 47)

To the rum add the zest, ginger, mace, grains of paradise, and anise.

Let the mixture sit in a wide-mouth, sterilized jar for 3 to 5 days; the thinner the zest, the less time needed. Strain the liquid into a sterilized, sealable jar, at least 16 ounces.

Heat the simple syrup with the leftover spice and zest mixture from macerating as a way to further extract flavors (you can skip this step if you like).

Let the simple syrup mixture cool; strain and blend with the rum you've already strained. Strain again if needed.

Store in a sterilized, airtight jar or bottle in a cool, dry place or the refrigerator for up to 8 weeks.

- Some recipes for falernum add lime juice, but that lowers the shelf life.

- Substitute 2 tablespoons almond syrup for some of the simple syrup to tiki it up.

- If you want to make history, lose all the spices except the ginger and sub them with a 21 whole clove salute. Enjoy the resultant subpar, yet historically accurate, drink.

CORN & OIL

The classic falernum cocktail, this drink must use good ingredients and your good falernum.

2 ounces good-quality rum
1 bar spoon (or more) Falernum
Lime wedges, to taste

Into an old-fashioned or rocks glass filled with ice, pour the rum and falernum, squeeze in a wedge or three of lime, and stir well.

VARIATIONS:

- Use a bigger glass and add a big splash of sparkling wine to make a Pop, Corn & Oil.

⤙ Berry Acid ⤚

Blackberries are everywhere in the Pacific Northwest, but natives see the vines as a scourge, even hiring gangs of goats to eradicate them. More than a decade here and I still freak out over blackberry season. Foraged blackberries are fantastic since the variety of ripeness and therefore flavor will be far greater than a store-bought pint—and cheaper. As in, free. When I make this recipe, I use large plastic food-safe containers. The ratio here is 4:3:1, berries, sugar, water, respectively.

Special equipment needed: cheesecloth and a large wide-mouth glass gallon jar.

Makes 6 cups

6 cups sugar
2½ tablespoons tartaric acid
8 cups fresh blackberries
2 cups water, distilled or filtered

Mix the sugar and tartaric acid together. Combine with the blackberries and water and pour into the sterilized glass jar; stir gently just to coat the berries. Cover with a lid and store in a very cool, dry place overnight or up to 48 hours. Turn the berries occasionally.

Strain the syrup through a double layer of cheesecloth, only lightly squeezing the berries.

Resterilize the glass jar and return the syrup mixture to it. Cover with 4 layers of fresh cheesecloth and secure with tape or string. Store in a very cool, dark place for 2 weeks to let the acid work its magic: the liquid will become extra thick and syrupy, with a little fizz to it.

Transfer to 2 sterilized wine bottles or small jars with super tight lids and store in the fridge.

- Use as you would a fruit syrup. To make a quick spritzer, mix 1 ounce of berry acid for every 4 to 6 ounces of soda water. To makeover a simple collins, sour, or even vodka lemonade, add ½ to 1 ounce of berry acid.

SLOW GIN FIZZ

Sloe denotes an actual berry, so work with me here. The average sloe gin on the market is no better than the average schnapps. Use your berry acid to approximate your own.

> 2 ounces gin
> Juice of ½ lemon
> 1 ounce Berry Acid
> 4 ounces soda water

Shake the gin, lemon juice, and berry acid with ice. Strain into a rocks glass packed with ice; add soda water to taste.

⋎ Cherry Bitters ⋏

This recipe highlights the sometimes-difference between using fresh (or fresh frozen) and dried fruit. Keep the spice-tinkering to a minimum or you'll likely end up with cherry cough syrup bitters. It's best used in a manhattan, drizzled over the cap of a traditional sour, or splashed into a brandy sidecar.

Makes 2 cups

2 cups dry whiskey (rye preferred)
1 cup tart, fresh cherries, or ½ cup dried, unsweetened cherries
1 vanilla bean, split and seeded
1 whole star anise
2 whole cloves
1 teaspoon horehound (see Note)
1 teaspoon fennel seed (see Note)

Combine the whiskey, cherries, vanilla bean, star anise, cloves, horehound, and fennel seed in a sterilized jar and seal tightly. Let the mixture macerate for 2 weeks in a cool, dark place, shaking gently daily.

Strain into one or more sterilized, airtight bottles and store at room temperature.

Note: For more mellow bitters, add the horehound and fennel seed after 1 week.

WHISKEY SODA, FASHIONED

Neither an old-fashioned nor a whiskey soda, but both at once.

1 orange slice
4 dashes Cherry Bitters
Sugar cube (optional)
1½ ounces or more whiskey
3 to 4 ounces soda water

Hit the slice of orange with the cherry bitters and then muddle it with the sugar cube. Add ice, whiskey, and soda water to taste.

∽ Fruit Purée ∾

I never use recipes for these anymore, kind of like making salad, really. You'll get the knack for it, too, after a few tries. This recipe presents just the basic ratio. Use peaches for the traditional Bellini purée.

Makes 2 cups

3 cups water
Zest and juice of 2 limes
1 cup sugar
1 teaspoon ground white pepper (optional)
2 teaspoons fresh thyme, minced (optional)
2 cups fresh fruit

Bring the water to a boil in a heavy-bottom saucepan (required so you don't scorch the fruit). Add the zest, sugar to taste depending on the fruit used, and white pepper (black is OK), and reduce the heat to simmer.

Add the fruit and, stirring often, simmer for up to 20 minutes. For the last 10 minutes, add the fresh thyme. Always add fresh herbs toward the end and spice and dried herbs with the sugar.

Remove from the heat, let cool, and purée in a blender. Based on the degree to which you want to strain the mixture, strain the purée through a sieve or colander to collect berry seeds and large bits of spice.

Store in sterilized, airtight jars or bottles in the fridge.

BELLINI

This is one of those drinks said to have originated in Harry's Bar in Venice, Italy, using white peach purée. It's simple and beautiful and requires one thing of you: don't eff up either ingredient. Use a bit of the fruit as garnish—a thin slice of peach or a single berry.

    2 ounces fresh Fruit Purée
    4 ounces prosecco or softer sparkling wine of very good quality

In a large champagne or small wine glass, pour in the purée; slowly pour in the sparkling wine. Stir gently to incorporate.

VARIATIONS:

- Marinate the fruit in a little dessert wine or liqueur overnight before puréeing.

⤙ Bitter Lemon Soda ⤚

You can buy Schweppes's Bitter Lemon soda, if you can find it. It is the magical beverage that takes the comfort of lemonade and crosses it with the bracing refreshment of tonic. This recipe is less bitter than the bottled variety. It's ideal with a brown amaro like Avera or any brown liquor, not to mention gin. Mix 1 ounce bitter lemon syrup to 6 ounces soda water.

Makes about 2½ cups

2¼ cups water
¾ cup sugar
Zest (with some pith) and juice of 4 lemons, divided
2 tablespoons powdered cinchona bark

Bring the water to a boil in a heavy-bottom saucepan. Add the sugar, stir until dissolved, and reduce the heat to medium low.

Add the lemon zest and the bark. Simmer for 30 minutes.

Remove from the heat and let cool. Double strain into a sterilized, airtight jar, add the lemon juice, and refrigerate for up to 6 weeks.

Use this tonic/lemonade hybrid in highballs. It goes with all major liquor groups.

VARIATIONS:

- Mix this syrup with distilled water and carbonate the entire thing.

<YOUR TOWN HERE> LEMONADE

Lynchburg lemonade is not just popular in Tennessee, even though the drink came from Jack Daniels's backyard. It's a long take on the whiskey sour, if you please. A Lynchburg lemonade, on average, comes out somewhere between a basic whiskey and lemonade long drink and a whiskey stone sour (a non-egg-white sour with added orange juice). Adjust the amounts depending on how much yardwork needs doing. By now, you must have a few concoctions in the cupboard. Remove the Tennessee and make this drink yours (unless you live in Tennessee, then carry on).

2 ounces whiskey
¾ ounce triple sec
2 ounces lemon juice
¾ ounce Simple Syrup (page 47)
½ ounce orange juice
Lemon or orange wedge

Combine all ingredients in a shaker with ice. Shake and strain into a large rocks glass filled with ice. Garnish with a lemon or orange wedge.

Vary at will.

Appendix 1:
ᕦ Mother Drinks ᕤ

In cooking, the basic sauces are referred to as "the mothers." All sauces branch out from the basics—bearnaise sauce is really just hollandaise sauce with herbs, for example. It's the same with cocktails; the basic recipes are few and the variations infinite. Use these recipes as a quick reference guide for employing projects in this book as well as random acts of drinking.

These recipes are chosen with an eye on the home bar and imbiber, not with bartending perspective in mind. Cousin cocktails are listed in parentheses. Plug in and play at will. Remember, few concoctions are so bad that they can't be saved with the addition of ice, soda, and an extra squeeze of lemon or lime.

MARTINI

People who get snobby about not using vermouth in their martini should just stop using the word and order their white liquor "cold and up." Martinis take vermouth, its aromatics and flavor making the drink. Make sure the vermouth is fresh or your own.

> 2½ ounces gin
> ½ ounce vermouth

Combine ingredients in a pint glass with ice. Stir, strain, and serve in your favorite glass with olives or a twist.

MANHATTAN (ROB ROY)

The original martini called for two parts gin, one part sweet vermouth, and a dash of orange bitters. Look familiar? That's a manhattan recipe if you change the liquor to brown. A Rob Roy subs Scotch for whiskey.

> 2 ounces whiskey
> 1 ounce sweet vermouth

Dash bitters (Angostura or orange)

Combine the whiskey, vermouth, and bitters in a pint glass and fill with ice. Stir and strain into a cocktail or favorite glass.

VARIATIONS:

- The Blackstrapped Manhattan (page 106) subs out the vermouth and bitters in this recipe for something richer and spicier. If you think a manhattan is too sweet, play with what you add instead of the standard sweet vermouth to make it less or differently so. Highlight different flavors in the drink with the bitters you use, like cherry, for example.

MARGARITA (SIDECAR)

An augmented daiquiri or gimlet, the margarita is the perfect expression of liquid refreshment.

2 ounces tequila, at least reposado in quality (see page 39)
½ ounce Cointreau, triple sec, or your orange Cello (page 117)
1 ounce lime juice
½ ounce Simple Syrup (page 47)
Salt (optional)

Combine the tequila, orange liqueur, lime juice, and simple syrup in a shaker filled with ice. Shake and strain into a rocks glass filled with ice. Rim the glass with salt first, if you like. Never serve it up. A warm margarita is an abomination.

VARIATIONS:

- A sidecar is basically a brandy margarita with lemon juice instead of lime and a sugar rim instead of salt. Use the same ratios above, replacing the tequila with your favorite brandy (or your own infused stuff).

DAIQUIRI (GIMLET)

A daiquiri is a gimlet with a little sweet added. Many gimlet recipes call for lime cordial, which is a sweetened lime syrup (Rose's being the ubiquitous example). Fresh lime juice is the only way to go.

> 2 ounces rum
> ¾ ounce fresh lime juice
> ¼ ounce Simple Syrup (page 47)

Combine the rum, lime juice, and simple syrup in a shaker filled with ice. Shake and strain into a pretty glass.

OLD-FASHIONED

This drink takes the edge off drinking whiskey on the rocks. If you're a fan, it's the perfect place to deploy your favorite bitters. I use rhubarb.

> 1 sugar cube
> 2 to 3 dashes bitters
> Splash of soda water
> 2 ounces whisk(e)y (bourbon, Scotch, brandy, or your own infusion)
> Orange slice and cherry (optional)

In a small rocks glass, place the sugar cube and soak with bitters. Muddle until sugar is mostly dissolved. Add soda water and whiskey and fill the glass with ice. Stir and garnish with an orange slice and respectable cherry (read: not neon maraschinos).

FRENCH 75 (TOM COLLINS)

Same idea as a Tom Collins, but with slightly different alcohol contents, the French 75 is a sleeper of a cocktail—strong, bracing, and sparkly.

> 1½ ounces gin
> 1 bar spoon Simple Syrup (page 47)
> ½ to ¾ ounce lime juice

3 or more ounces sparkling wine
Lime peel

Combine the gin, simple syrup, and lime juice in a shaker and fill with ice. Shake and strain into a cocktail or simple rocks glass. Top with sparkling wine. Garnish with a lime peel.

The float of bubbly is what makes a French 75; otherwise it's just a version of a gin daiquiri. There are endless amounts of cocktail recipes toying with the combination of simple syrup, citrus juice, and a spirit. Many of these add a liqueur into the mix (hello, margarita). Add soda water instead of sparkling wine, and you have a collins.

VARIATIONS:

- To make a Tom Collins, start with the above rations of gin, lime, and simple syrup and pour it over ice packed into a 10- to 12-ounce glass. Instead of sparkling wine, top off the glass with soda water.

SOUR (SEE PAGE 139)

This drink is only limited by your imagination and bar stock.

HIGHBALL

A highball is the most underappreciated of drinks. Whiskey and soda, gin and tonic, Dark and Stormy (rum and ginger ale)—this is a category of drinks that focuses on one spirit with the addition of a mixer. It's drinking minimalism. Sometimes, you'll make an infusion that you don't want to cover up with too many other ingredients or flavors. Highball it.

1½ ounces liquor
4 to 6 ounces mixer

Combine the liquor and mixer in a rocks glass packed with ice.

MINT JULEP

Similar to a mojito, the julep is the better, stronger drink.

7 fresh mint leaves (plus sprig for garnish)
1 bar spoon sugar (preferably superfine)
2½ ounces bourbon

In a large or tall rocks glass, muddle mint with the sugar and a splash of water. You want to use the sugar to scour the surface of the mint leaves and release all the oils. Add the bourbon, then fill the glass with ice and stir. Garnish with a sprig of mint.

MOJITO

To make a mojito, you're doing the same thing, with more of a highball ratio of spirit to mixer, and adding lime.

7 mint leaves
½ ounce Simple Syrup (page 47)
2 lime wedges
1½ ounces rum
3 to 4 ounces soda water

Follow the above instructions (adding lime to muddling process) and finish by topping with soda water.

Variations:

- If you're a fan of this drink, use your favorite bourbon in the recipe for Minted Rum (page 163). You can sub in basil or cilantro for a weirder, more savory take on the drink.

PLUG-N-PLAY COCKTAIL RATIO

In answer to "what do I do with this?" start here. Just as a basic salad dressing can begin with a ratio of oil to vinegar to accent flavor, begin cocktail experimentation by determining your 1. base spirit, 2. adjunct flavor or liqueur, and 3. accent (acid or amaro).

   2 ounces base spirit
   ½ to ¾ ounce liqueur or adjunct (vermouth, etc.), depending
      on intensity
   ¼ to ½ ounce accent (citrus, sour or amaro)
   Dash of bitters (optional)

Combine all ingredients in a pint glass and fill with ice. Stir or shake, then strain into your favorite, most appropriate glass with or without ice.

Appendix 2:
ᴧ A Quickie Glossary ᴧ

Brown liquor:
This is a catchall phrase to describe bourbon, whiskey, whisky, Scotch, and their like. In other words, aged grain spirits. The term orbits around whisk(e)y and is sometimes used for ease of description in writing.

Dash:
A dash of bitters involves a one-flick motion with the bottle, just as you would soy sauce or hot sauce. You do this all the time. In the bar, we keep the bitters bottle three-quarters full for consistent dashing.

Fining:
Think of the act of fining the same as you would straining, just on a much smaller level of particles. You're removing the fine particles. This word is common in winemaking, and I use it here in conjunction with clarifying infusions with coffee filters.

Growler:
A growler is a ½-gallon jug with a tiny handle at the neck. It is a common way to purchase tap beer for takeaway from breweries. It would be the perfect size for infusions if it didn't have such a tiny neck.

Long drink:
A long drink is the same concept as a tall latte. Same amount of high-octane ingredients, more mixer.

Muddle:
A muddler looks like a small baseball bat. When muddling, you take one end of the bat and press/lightly crush the ingredients. In a mojito, for example, you're tearing the mint oil free by muddling it with sugar, which acts as the scrub. You will often see some bartenders working a muddler as if they were churning butter on crack. This is an abusive act, unless you like mint pesto in your mojito.

Rasp:
A microplaner is a fancy rasp. It's a handheld tool that removes pieces of an object in shavings, like a grater. The verb is the act of removal.

Shake vs. stir:
OK, this is self-explanatory but I needed to call this out somewhere. In general, you stir drinks that are all booze (manhattans, martinis) and you shake drinks that have citrus or other elements, but feel free to shake OR stir at will.

Spent vanilla beans:
There are many ways to use a vanilla bean. The most desired part is the little inner black bits you are used to seeing in vanilla ice cream. You split the bean and scrap it. Then you can use just the bean steeped in liquid to add more vanilla flavor. Once you've done this, the bean is spent. You can use it again steeped in liquid (or soaked in alcohol) to impart vanilla flavor and aroma to a far mellower degree.

Zest vs. peel vs. rind:
Zest is the colorful part of the citrus skin only, where all the aromatic oils live. A peel refers to a part of the citrus skin that includes the colorful zest and pith below. It can be of any size and shape. Rind means the same thing as peel, though this term is more often used with fruit that has a stiffer outer shell (like melon).

⌁ Resources ⌁

These are some of my favorite and trusted sources.

Bar & Kitchen Equipment
Check with your local kitchen and/or restaurant supply store, or try the following online (or near you):

www.williams-sonoma.com

www.surlatable.com

www.amazon.com

Bottles & Jars
Always check your local hardware store for canning jars; they all stock them.

For small bottles and jars for bitters—and also eyedroppers—and presentation, try Specialty Bottle at www.specialtybottle.com.

Herbs & Spices
Tenzing Momo
93 Pike Street, in the Economy Building
Seattle's Pike Place Market
www.tenzingmomo.com

World Spice Merchants
1509 Western Avenue
Seattle's Pike Place Market
www.worldspice.com

Sugarpill Apothecary
900 East Pine Street
Seattle's Capitol Hill neighborhood
www.sugarpillseattle.com

The Souk
1916 Pike Place #11
Seattle's Pike Place Market

Preserving

For further information on preserving and canning, visit my friend Brooke's most excellent site: www.learningtopreserve.com.

Homebrewing (beer, mead, sodas . . .)

The website www.homebrew.com is a great place to start for a novice, should some of the recipes in this book give you a new hobby.

ᴧ Index ᴧ